MEANT

for **MORE**

*Stop Secretly Struggling and Become a
Force to Be Reckoned With*

MIA HEWETT

Meant For More
Stop Secretly Struggling and Become a Force to Be Reckoned With

Difference Press, Washington, D.C., USA
Copyright © Mia Hewett, 2019

ISBN: 978-1-68309-242-1

Cover Design: Jennifer Stimson
Editing: Moriah Howell
Author's photo courtesy of Nikki Johnson-Incandela
Cover Photo Courtesy of Caroline White

DP
DIFFERENCE
PRESS

Advance Praise

$\mathcal{T}$his book is powerful. It helps the reader see, in themselves, what is really preventing them from living their potential. And, it's not what you think. This will have you wake up to the truth that is already within you.

> — WELDON LONG, *New York Times Bestselling Author*

Mia Hewett's Meant for More guides you through an epic journey of self-discovery that is available to us all. Her book demystifies the limitations operating in your life while awakening you to the Universe operating within. Profound!

> — MATT FUREY, *Author of Theatre of the Mind, President, Psycho-Cybernetics Foundation*

This book is earth shattering! It will change how you see the world, yourself, and what you're capable of. And it's all so simple. Mia figured out a way to allow you to shift your perception and alter your reality all with so much ease, excitement, and love. She is truly such a gift, and this book is the most generous contribution she could give us all.

> — DR. NEDA HOVAIZI

This book is full of so much wisdom! Sometimes we have the good fortune of meeting someone that can totally change how we see the world and ourselves. That is what happened when I met Mia. If you're struggling, and you know you are Meant for More, then this is the book for you!

— RUTH LEWIS-TRATCH, *Entrepreneur And Network Marketing Professional*

Amazing book! I wish I knew Mia many years ago. I had been living in the deepest of fogs and finally feel the fog clearing! Mia helped me Align what I want with my thoughts, emotions, and actions. I highly suggest you read this book.

— DR. SHAHRZAD KHORASHADI, *DMD, Harvard University*

Mia Hewett is a powerhouse in the coaching and personal development space. There are very few people in the world that are dedicated to her craft like she is. Mia walks the walk, and she gets results. Everyone's lives will be richer when they get a copy of Meant for More in their hands, so don't wait another second. Go get yourself this book today.

— DAVE SCATCHARD, *Peak Performance Coach, Former NHL Hockey Player*

Mia has a gift of helping others identify and heal the true cause of what holds them back from reaching their full potential. Mia is nothing less than honest, real, and raw. A must read.

— AMANDA PORTILLO, *CEO & Career Coach*

Mia quickly, and efficiently demystifies any obstacles that are keeping you from your greatness. This book allows you to identify and then tackle all your issues from the root. She has an amazing gift and has shared it with such grace and clarity for everyone who truly believes they are Meant for More.

— SANKEETHA SELVARAJAH, ESQ.

Table of Contents

CHAPTER 9
How to Use Your Power to Create Your Reality Intentionally 143

Author's Note

This book is dedicated to humanity, the evolution of consciousness, and for the infinite expansion of love and connection everywhere.

It is a love letter from my soul to yours, from my higher self to my younger self. It's the book I had always been looking for and could never find that I would've loved for someone to have given me a long time ago.

I have used my own life story in hopes that more people may realize how they too can stop secretly struggling, awaken to their full potential, to their own Truth, and be the confident leaders they were born to be.

In it, I share fundamental Truths, and key principles through a process I call Aligned Intelligence ™. I have found that when we raise our conscious level of awareness and understanding of how life really works and then learn as humans, how we function in actuality, our old perceptions of reality lose their grip, causing a permanent paradigm shift, transforming our reality.

In its place is our natural state of clarity, well-being, and peace of mind.

In this clarity, it's easy for you to access your true power, tap into your own inner wisdom, inner guidance, and hidden Truth – the beauty of who you really are.

Additionally, throughout this book, I've used many examples from my personal clients' lives. However, to ensure their privacy and confidentiality, I've changed their names and minor details of their experiences where appropriate to do so.

My only request is if this book touches your heart, and as you see things newly, I would be honored and grateful if you would pass it on by sharing it with others so that they too may awaken to their own inner wisdom, their own inner guidance, and their own inner Truth.

For all any of us ever have to do is to suspend our doubts and reasons long enough to allow the light and Truth to shine through so that it becomes our reality.

There is great love here for you!

I believe in you!

INTRODUCTION

IS THIS BOOK FOR YOU?

I grew up poor and when I was about thirteen years old, my dog Macho, whom I loved dearly, died because our house was so infested with fleas that they literally sucked the blood out of him.

It broke my heart.

That day I made a decision that I would never be poor again. At the time I didn't know how or what I was going to do, but I knew that I would never have a child or animal that I could not afford to take care of.

I later went on to co-own and operate a multi-million dollar insurance company for twenty-four years, and I had what society would call success, yet inside I felt like a failure. I ran all the major marathons in the world: New York, Chicago, Boston, Berlin, and London thinking I was going to arrive just as soon as I accomplished the next goal, the next milestone, but my arrival never came. All I kept feeling was empty like something was missing, and I just could not put my finger on it. I'd smile and put on a happy face to the world, but internally, I was lost. And to make matters worse, my dreams often threatened others, even some of my own family. This left me always feeling like no one gets me and I am alone.

I was great at insurance, but I didn't honestly feel like I was living my purpose. My clients and staff used to always tell me "you're in the wrong profession; you should've been in personal development; you should've been a coach." And although I loved the idea of that, I felt internally conflicted between what I thought I needed to do for my family versus what I truly wanted to do.

Have you ever felt that way?

I mean, if not me, who? Right? At forty-four, I felt conflicted between these two sides of myself:

- I knew I wanted to play a bigger game in the world, but I also felt comfortable and therefore safer to just keep making the money I already knew how to make.

- I knew I wanted to share my knowledge and wisdom, but I worried about what people might think about me.

- I knew I wanted to be my unique self, but I also wanted to fit in and be liked.

- I knew I wanted to be seen and recognized for doing great work but standing out in the "limelight" was scary.

- I knew I wanted to be confident, but certain people intimidated the crap out of me, which left me feeling paralyzed or talking incessantly.

With all of these mixed feelings, I consistently felt overwhelmed, stuck, stopped, and constantly struggling thinking, 'what is wrong with me?'

At forty-four, I thought it was too late for me to do something new as I didn't know how I would do it. I also felt it would take way too long and be too painful. Could I even handle it? What if I failed? What would my family think of me? Although I felt like I was "right" in hindsight, I was wrong. And my discovery on how I was wrong is what allowed me to set myself free and develop a proven methodology to help all others do the same. Easily.

I now live an incredible life, living my life's purpose and doing what I am most passionate about, having the most amazing experiences with an incredible partner who allows me the space to play big and be fully me. I genuinely love my life, and it keeps expanding beautifully.

So how did I get here?

What I have found, in not only analyzing my own successes, but in interviewing and working with countless others; from best-selling authors like Jack Canfield and Mel Robbins, to billionaires Martin Franklin and Jeff Hoffman, and many more, is that every single person had each mastered, in their own way, the same attributes in achieving their potential. They did it by evolving their way of being and taking action from a new conscious awareness and understanding to achieve their potential and live their results. Even if they could not explicitly describe how they did it, they would all tell me things like "I just knew."

What did they know? How can others tap into that? Why is it that, with SO many programs and motivational speakers out there, why was only 2-5% of people achieving extraordinary results?

How was it that I was successful yet I still felt like a failure?

I knew there had to be a better way. There had to be something missing, and I set out to discover it. Not only for myself but also for anyone who has always known they were 'Meant For More.' I have now worked with tons of people and understand precisely what works and what doesn't. And I am so excited to let you in on what successful people know, that they often cannot explain, so that you can understand it too! I use a methodology I call my Aligned Intelligence Method™ or A.I.M. It is simple, yet profound, as wisdom always *is*.

Many of my clients are seasoned veterans, highly intelligent, and financially successful. They've taken courses, hired the best business and life coaches, gone to years of therapy, hired consultants, and still felt like something was missing. When they learned the very methodology this book demonstrates, their results transformed in days or weeks. Often hitting their yearlong goals in as little as the first couple of months and some in a matter of weeks.

Meant For More' is for you if you've ever felt like you were meant for more but didn't know why you are not living it. It is a story of one woman's journey to discover what she was missing. And, this is not a book just for women since many of my clients are Men. It is for anyone that knows they are 'Meant For More' and have not yet been able to live their Unlimited Potential. This book was written to bring this technology to the world, to you.

This book is dedicated to setting you free.

CHAPTER 1

INCEPTION – THE ORIGIN OF AN IDEA

"The tragedy of life is not death, rather it is what we allow to die within us while we live."
– NORMAN COUSINS

I think I hear my father calling me...

I don't answer right away for I am busy. I am playing in my room.

At five years old, my favorite doll is Baby Steps, and I am frustrated that I've gotten her hair wet in the bath last night and now I am struggling to untangle the rat nest I've created.

I hear him again: "Sue Marie! Are you back there?" I know from the sound of his voice he means business because I just heard him call me by my middle name. A name I forget I even have until I've done something wrong.

Why is he calling me? I think to myself as I start to feel anxious, I have this nervous feeling, as all the hair on the back of my neck stands up.

I know I have to answer.

Of all the people I fear in my house, my father is the one who scares me the most as I can never tell when something is going to set him off.

In one moment, he can be telling the funniest story, reenacting it in such a way that I have to hold my legs together not to pee myself. And then, in the next moment, something will set him off, and someone will get hurt, which usually seemed to be me!

I quickly jumped to my feet. "Coming!" I say, fearing his belt.

As I come around the corner of my room, I can see him from across the sunken living room floor, standing there with his hands on his hips.

There is something in the way he is standing that feels off to me, yet I can't quite put my finger on it.

I am searching my mind. *What have I done?* I can't think of anything. *Why is he calling me?*

"Yes?" I say.

"Come here. I want us to go outside," he says.

"Ok, but why?" I ask, trying to hide that I am scared.

In the past, whenever he would go outside, he would always take my sister Ann. She is Dad's favorite.

As the oldest, Ann is the boy Dad never had.

What Ann thinks looks like fun and will be an adventure, I think looks scary and means I most likely will die.

If Ann is the tomboy, then I am definitely the girly girl.

He doesn't answer me.

"Dad?" I say, my voice trembling.

"I want us to spend some time together you and me."

Really? I think. *Dad wants to spend time with me?*

Wow! I feel so special. I am sure Ann is going to be mad he took me.

I squeeze Baby Steps, giving her the biggest bear hug I can muster, and tell her, "Get ready. We are going on an adventure."

Outside, I instantly feel the warm sun on my skin as this day feels so special; my dad chose me. I say that to myself again, smiling as I walk behind him to the farmhouse.

"Which one of these is your favorite?" Dad asks, pointing at our free-ranging chickens.

Well, that's easy, I think to myself. "That one!" I say. Pointing at Henny Penny.

Of all the chickens we have on our farm, she is my absolute favorite. Anytime I go outside, she'll immediately come over to see what I'm doing, as she loves it when I dig up worms for her to eat.

"Good," I hear my father say. "Then she's the one we are going to kill today."

Wait! What!? My mind starts to spin out of control; I am so confused as I try to think about all the different ways or the different things I might say to be able to stop this from happening. I start screaming, but it sounds like it is coming from someone else. I hear it again, and realize it's me.

"No, no, no! No! *No!*" I yell. What have I done?! Tears start flowing down my cheeks. I have done something horrible; this is all my fault!

I freeze inside. I feel my mind going blank.

At that moment, life as I know it forever changes.

CHAPTER 2

YOUR GREATEST POWER

"Nothing happens unless something is moved."
– ALBERT EINSTEIN

Thirty years later, it is another cold winter day in Boston and I am at Tatte's Bakery & Café, a favorite spot among the locals. From my car I can see everyone has crammed inside, except for two extremists who are refusing to accept how cold it is. They are eating their breakfast outside as if it is eighty degrees, completely oblivious to the twenty-one-degree condition that my car's temperature gauge is showing me.

As someone who was born in Florida and raised in South America, I will never understand how they do that. I wonder if they are just born this way? I make a mental note to steer clear of them when I run for the front door, just in case they are as hostile as the weather feels. I laugh at how easily I can amuse myself.

As I continue to watch these two people, I wonder when they learned to go against the status quo and what is it that makes this type of person different? What is it that makes them be unapologetically themselves?

I've always wondered how to become the latter as it seems they are a rare breed.

In all my life, I can only think of one person who seems to exude this type of quality, and I had only just met her: my friend, Neda. It's like she operates on a completely different set of rules.

Clearly not the rules I've been given. If they gave out degrees in surviving, I would definitely be among the experts.

I've only known life from surviving it, starting from when I was six years old and my parents moved my sisters and me to a rural area in South America called Puerto La Cruz. My father, who was Venezuelan, had never taught us any Spanish. The result of this was so traumatic for my sisters and me when we attended a Venezuelan school where only Spanish was spoken. One day when we had come home from school without our younger sister, our mother asked us frantically, "Where is your sister?"

We told her we didn't know; she wasn't where we were supposed to meet. My mother, full of fear, took us back to our school, only to find our little sister coming out of the school crying hysterically.

My mother asked her, "What happened?"

She sobbed, "I got locked in the bathroom!"

My mother asked her, "Well, why didn't you scream?"

She said, *"Because I don't speak Spanish!"*

Ha! A good rule of thumb to remember: if you are ever going to put your English-speaking children in an all Spanish-speaking school, you may want to teach them survival 101 by explaining that screaming, means '*Help!*' in any language.

As a child, I survived every day at school. Not only because no one spoke any English, but because on top of that, they had never seen a white girl before. This made them either extremely freaked out by my appearance or extremely curious, which meant they would constantly want to touch my hair or feel my skin. To survive this, I would tell myself it would soon be over, not to move, because if I did, they would turn it into a game of chase and touch which somehow always felt worse. I pretended I was invisible with each pass of their hands. Some of them were extremely fearful because they didn't understand who or what I was. It was as if I was some freak of nature.

I watched as they pointed at me, said things I didn't understand, and then they would all laugh. I felt so alone, so different, like no one understood me.

I'd survived the brutal killing of a pig when my family was invited to a friend's BBQ. I cried inside, terrified, as I watched kids my age chase and kill a pig by throwing stones at its head until they smashed its skull. A ritual the natives found entertaining for all their friends and family. I had nightmares for weeks hearing that pig scream.

I'd survived almost drowning. My father took my sisters and I camping, and we came to a section in the trail where there was a rapidly moving river. My older sister complained that she wished she could go swimming; hearing that, my father decided that everyone would go swimming that day. Against my wishes and while I was begging and crying, he tied a rope around my waist and threw me into the class-four rapids and then got to decide when I'd gone under enough times that he felt it was time to pull me back in. I thought I would die that day.

I'd survived my father driving drunk. One night when I was really young, my parents had taken my sisters and me with them to a party where my dad had too much to drink. Driving home he started swerving all over the road. The other cars kept honking incessantly and yelled obscenities at us, while my sisters and I all held hands crying in the back seat. I remember feeling so scared and then later angry with my mother for not making my father stop the car and let her drive. I only learned later, as an adult, that she was too afraid if she said something, he would get even angrier and do something out of spite, and hurt us all or worse, kill us.

I'd survived my parents' divorce. My father got caught sleeping with the woman next door and so my mother packed all of us kids up and moved us back to Florida. There, once again, I felt like I didn't fit in. At thirteen, the kids in Florida were into sex, drugs, and rock-n-roll—things I had never heard of since I had just come from the jungle where we were catching tarantulas, I had a pet monkey, and where I was doing dead ant ceremonies with my friends.

I'd survived being poor – immediately after my parents' divorce and our subsequent move back to the United States my mother became the sole provider for four kids on a beginning teacher's salary. I can often remember going to bed hungry, as there never seemed to be enough food in our house and the food we did have always had bugs in it. My mother, trying to make light of our situation, would always tell us "don't worry, they are just good protein."

I'd survived being beat up in middle school – one day when I walked into typing; I felt a tap on my shoulder. When I turned around, I saw a girl who I'd never seen before. She started beating the crap out of me by punching me repeatedly in my mouth. I remember being in shock, just staring at her, so confused at the hatred coming from her eyes. I heard all the kids screaming "Hit Her! Hit Her!" In truth they could've been rooting for me to defend myself, but I thought they were rooting for her to kill me. I froze in terror.

I only learned later on in the dean's office that the reason she beat me up was because she thought I was stuck up as I had never said a word to her. It had never occurred to me before that day that my shyness could have ever been misinterpreted in that way.

I had survived these experiences and events and many, many, more... all before my seventeenth birthday.

I remembered my beautiful friend Tina, saying to me years later, "Sue, you are the most courageous girl I know!"

To which I replied, "No, I am just the ultimate survivor you know. Ha. I am like a coyote." I explained, "I've just learned how to survive in any situation, and under all circumstances."[1]

As I sit here now, in my beautiful silver Range Rover, I have so much appreciation for just how far I've come; yet I can't help but feel that I was meant for so much more.

I glance around the street where my car is parked to see if I can see her. *I don't think she's here, yet,* I think to myself. Neda is one of the only friends I've made since I moved here six months ago.

I take a long deep breath, inhaling as much as I can to brace myself from the cold and then I open the car door and run as fast as I can into the café, thanking God that there was no black ice along the way.

Once inside, I immediately get in line, and then I quickly scan the café to see if I recognize anyone. I notice a few people that Neda had previously pointed out to me.

Bostonians are by far some of the toughest people I've ever met.

As someone who has lived in other countries and different parts of the United States, most often I've heard people say that they think New Yorkers are among the toughest, but when I was running our insurance agency, a lot of my clients were New Yorkers, and I would completely disagree. In general, New Yorkers are just more confrontational, which in the beginning of my career used to scare the shit out of me. Eventually I grew really fond of them because I'd know exactly where I stood with them and I liked that. Once they knew they could trust me because I always did what I said I was going to do, they became my most loyal customers and my best referral sources. Bostonians, on the other hand, are an entirely different breed.

In general, they're highly cynical, do not trust anyone, and most often won't respond at all, never giving you an opportunity to prove you're trustworthy.

Neda once explained, "It takes them longer here, but once you're in, you're *in*! Be patient."

I look around and wonder, "Why do I live here?"

"Your usual?" a firm voice startles me back into reality. "A twelve-ounce latte with an extra shot, no foam," Sara says without smiling from behind the counter.

"Yes, thank you, Sara," I say, smiling at her, attempting to see if I could break her stoicism, but she doesn't bite.

She hands me my latte just in time for me to grab two seats from a couple that are just leaving. I sit; reflecting on my life, and glance down at my coffee, noticing the perfect heart the barista has just made. I laugh out loud at the irony. Ha!

"Hi, Sue!"

I look up and see Neda. "Hey, beautiful!" I say.

Neda is one of the most beautiful Persian girls I've ever met. She looks like she could be related to the Kardashians. She was born in Boston but grew up in Virginia and is just the most genuinely nice person, yet very firm and confident in herself. She's a thirty-four-year-old entrepreneur who owns two successful businesses, all while having two children under the age of five. And somehow, miraculously, she still has time to meet me for a coffee even though she doesn't drink it, but just because she likes the idea of it.

"How are you?" she asks me.

"I'm alright," I say unconvincingly.

"Okay, now *really*, how are you?" she says.

Neda has this unique ability to see right through what someone is saying, and since I know this, it's useless for me to even try to hide it. I say, "Well, actually I feel like I've hit a plateau, and I hate feeling this way."

"Really? Tell me more," she says.

"Well, you know I've co-owned an insurance company and have helped grow it to a multi-million dollar company, and now I am consulting, but I know that I was meant for so much more and I don't know how to get there."

"I know that's frustrating," Neda says compassionately.

"Yes, it is! It's frustrating, because I think I should be able to figure this out. I mean I am a really smart person."

"I am curious, Sue, what do you think you are most frustrated about?" Neda asks.

"I just want to take the success I am already having and scale it in a much bigger way, you know? By making a bigger impact in the world. I know that I have it in me, but I don't know what I am missing."

"How big do you want to take this?" Neda asks curiously.

"Like national." Hearing myself say that out loud, I feel a sort of tremor inside of me. "You see, in all my companies I've always been the one behind the scenes, and I feel like this would be all 'me', you know?"

"Yes," Neda says.

"And to be honest, I lead a really freaking great life! So there is a part of me that feels guilty, like why can't I just be happy? Why do I always have to push for more, when I have so much? And then there is another part of me that wonders how long I can keep all this up."

"Sometimes our success is our greatest limiting belief," Neda says.

"That's so true! I mean, I know by society's standards that I am what's considered a success, so why do I feel like such a failure?" I look away for a moment to gather my thoughts. "And then I have another part of me that says why can't I just accept the life I have? I mean, this is good, right?"

Neda's just looking at me with her incredible brown eyes, which snaps me back into the present moment as I realize I've been talking nonstop about myself since she sat down.

"Oh! I am so sorry," I say. "I just emotionally vomited all over you. This is probably not even making much sense to you." I shake my head, embarrassed for having carried on this way. I then ask her, "How are your kids? Trying to change the topic to be more about her and something that sounds way more pleasant.

Neda just keeps on smiling as if she knows something I don't know.

I look at her, waiting for her to say something. Finally, when I can't take it anymore, I say, "What? Why are you smiling at me like this?"

"Sue, you have no idea just how familiar this all sounds to me," she says. "I used to feel the exact same way!"

"What? You? Really?" I am genuinely shocked and, quite honestly, a bit confused. "How's that possible? You are always so self-assured and so confident!"

I've always looked at Neda as the one person who just had the "it" factor. The kind that hasn't had to struggle. The kind that just appears like they are just born with it. Born with a presence about them in the way they act, look and sound, like they always just know exactly how to be.

"Yes," she says. "I used to struggle, always feeling like I was just grinding away, like I was failing somehow at life. I mean, I feel really fortunate that I've always had amazing parents, and that they've always taught me to believe that I can accomplish anything I put my mind to but I've always felt like I was meant for so much more. Then after my babies were born and I gained some extra weight, I started feeling like I wasn't moving forward anymore, like I wasn't being me. That's when I started doubting myself and wondering if I'd ever reach my true potential. I mean I knew I was smart, so why couldn't I just figure this out?"

"Oh my gosh, that's exactly how I feel," I say, dumbfounded.

She nods. "Yes, until someone introduced me to my mentor, who opened my eyes so I could see things I'd never seen before."

"Really? Who is that?" I ask, wondering if that is really even possible, but I keep smiling so I don't hurt her feelings.

Neda laughs. "I know this sounds a bit far-fetched and out there, but I'm going to give you her phone number. She's pretty amazing, and you can choose to call her or not. But if you do... well, let me just tell you now, your life will forever change." She reaches into her purse.

Now I'm really intrigued. I mean, how could someone as confident as Neda think so highly of this person?

Neda says, "All I can say is that for me it has been life changing. Not only for how I look at business, but how she gave me permission to unapologetically realize my full potential." Finding her phone in her purse, she pulls it out and texts me the woman's contact information. "Her name is Mia and she's is one of the best-kept secrets. She's like the Oprah of business and life all in one. A good friend of mine referred her to me a few years ago when I felt lost, and she changed my life. And now, I want to pay it forward and do the same for you."

My phone buzzes with Neda's text. I feel both excited and doubtful, as I'm an avid reader who has spent a lifetime doing trainings, hiring the best personal development coaches in the industry, and learning from top mentors. What could this one person really teach me that I don't already know? After all, I know how to reframe my mind, be careful with the words I choose, and think positively. At the same time, I still couldn't say I feel any less confused or that I had really reached anywhere near my potential.

In fact, quite the opposite. I actually feel at times more overwhelmed and more frustrated with myself. If I know so much, then why am I not living my potential? I just can't see how this one person is *really* going to be all that different. I mean, if she's so great, why hasn't everyone heard of her? I wasn't even sure how I would fit this into my already tight schedule of clients.

Neda interrupts my thoughts by saying, "She's created her own methodology and technology when nothing else she tried had worked for her before, and it's not like anything you've ever experienced. She combines so many different things together: incredible business knowledge, spirituality, psychology, science, forward thinking, and, above all else, she is just a genuinely good person."

"How do you always know what I am thinking? Or is it that my skepticism is just written all over my face?" I laugh, thinking that maybe I am not all that different from these Bostonians after all. Ha!

"Because I used to think just like you," Neda says, laughing. "Trust me, I was hesitant at first, too. But what I am confident about is that I would do it again in a heartbeat – just five years earlier! She doesn't work with just anyone. If she doesn't think it's a fit, she will refer you out. She's a real force. Either way, it's your call. I just know if you work with her it will be the best investment you will ever make in yourself because, as she's taught me, *success is an inside job before it will ever become an outside reality. And your greatest power comes from you choosing, so choose wisely.*"

Neda's words crack a small piece off my hardened exterior shell. I can see there is real truth in what she is saying. She gets up, gives me a big hug, and says, "I've gotta run. There is a reason you are seeking this; just listen to your inner voice. It knows the right thing for you. And, if you do happen to call her, tell her I send my love as I think about her every day!" And just like that, she's out the door.

I stare at my phone and then back at my leftover coffee.

Processing what Neda just said, I take another sip of my now-distorted heart. It looks like how I feel – a swirl of emotions all tangled up.

I grab a spoon off the table and proceed to stir it. How could this one person really be able to teach me anything new that I don't already know? I mean, I've lived a really diverse life, one that I don't feel most people get. I've known poverty, I've known tremendous wealth, and I have so much that I should be grateful for, and yet I always feel somehow that I am not enough. I swallow the last sip of my coffee, put on my coat, grab my purse, and go out the door.

Sitting back in my car, I take another look at my phone, thinking on what Neda had said. My mind is still flooded with doubt; I think maybe I just need to admit that my big dreams are not going to fit my reality.

Yet, I just can't get out of my head how confident Neda always is and how easy she makes business and life look.

Can a person really be that happy *and* successful? What else has this mentor taught her? I sigh deeply. What's the worst that could happen? I think to myself...I don't want to make another bad decision and waste my money. With that thought, I toss my phone into my purse and drive off.

Later that night, I feel more anxious than usual. I try to distract myself, so I decide to binge-watch my favorite episodes of *Game of Thrones*. How am I ever going to survive when this show ends? I don't think George R. R. Martin knows how much this show has been my favorite fix. I laugh at my thoughts. It's getting late and I really need to go to bed. I convince myself to just watch one more episode.

Before I know it, it's 1:30 a.m. and I know I will not be getting up at 5:30 like I had promised myself. I wash my face and get under the covers and stare at the ceiling. Tossing and turning, I eventually fall asleep.

I find myself sitting on a beautiful beach surrounded by a crowd of people. It looks so familiar... where have I seen this before? My mind starts racing, searching for the connection, and then it comes to me: oh! Yes, of course, this is like the beach in *Games of Thrones*. It has these tall cliffs of jagged mountains right next to the ocean like the one by the castle Dragonstone. I hear people's voices but I can't make out what they're saying, and for a moment, a quiet peace comes over me as I feel the warmth of the sun all over my body. I decide to lie back down. I close my eyes and soak in the moment.

Then in the very next second, I notice there is a dead silence. I am confused – how did it get so quiet? I open my eyes and look around, but there is no one here. I stand up, and look up and down both sides of the beach, but still there's no one around. What happened? Did I fall asleep? I start to panic and feel like screaming, but I am afraid. What if screaming is the wrong thing to do? How will I survive this? I feel so scared. I am all alone. I must've done something awful. I drop down to my knees, feeling the sand around my skin, and put my head in my hands. I begin to cry uncontrollably. My heart feels so constricted in my chest that I can't catch my breath. I don't know what to do. I feel frozen inside and my mind starts to go blank and then I wake up.

Wow. I realize it was all a dream. For a moment, it all felt so real.

I sit up and look around and then grab my phone off the nightstand, realizing it's 7:43 a.m. I've overslept; I check my alarm and realize I had mistakenly set it for p.m. instead of a.m.

I think about Mel Robbins's 5 Second Rule. I hear her voice in my head saying, "If you have an instinct to act, you must physically move within five seconds or your brain will kill it," and before I can change my mind, I grab my phone, open Neda's last text, and push the send button on the call icon.

"Hi, this is Mia," the voice on the other end says.

I'm shocked that someone had actually answered. Mia's voice sounds firm, grounded; yet warm and inviting. "Oh! Hi, this is Sue, um, I know this is a bit early... Well, actually, I didn't really expect anyone to answer and I was given your number from a friend. Oh, I'm sorry, is this a bad time to talk?" I realize I'm rambling, and that's not the first impression I want to make with this woman.

"Absolutely not, Sue. I am happy you called. How may I help you?" she says, sounding genuinely curious and trusting.

I pause for a second, enjoying this feeling of comfort coming from this total stranger. I'm not used to feeling this comfortable with someone I've only just met. I take a deep breath and calm myself. "Mia, I am not sure if you can help me, but a good friend of mine, Neda, speaks really highly of you, and how you've helped her, so I thought I should call you."

"Ah, of course, Neda is amazing," Mia says.

Surprisingly, I start telling her everything I've been struggling with; I tell her about the insurance company and the business I've had since then. I even start telling her more personal things.

"Well, you see, I am divorced, my kids are grown, and I went from being this highly successful business woman with my ex-husband to now being in business for myself and I feel like I am stuck. Like, I know I'm meant for more, but I don't know how to achieve it? And on top of that, I feel burned-out, like I am spinning all these plates and at any moment they are all just going to come crumbling down." It feels so good to just say this out loud that I make myself say what I really don't want to tell her: "And on top of all that, I feel like a failure because my success has never been quite what I want. With each day I am finding it even more and more difficult to motivate myself to do things I know I should be doing."

I can't believe I admitted this to a total stranger. It feels both freeing and terrifying. But I am tired... exhausted, really.

The sound of Mia's voice snaps me out of my thoughts. "Well, the good news is, Sue, that you are actually not alone. *One of the biggest mistaken beliefs we have in our society is that we feel that in order to be successful we can't have any weaknesses.*[2]

"We actually learned this as children. It is often just implied in the background, either when we are being punished by a parent, scolded by a teacher, or even teased by our own friends. Either way, we learn that it's not ok to have any kind of weaknesses. Would you say that is how you are feeling? Like there is something wrong with you if you feel weak?" Mia asks.

"I've never thought of it that way, but now that you say it like that, yes," I answer. "I feel it's wrong. I should just be able to figure this out."

"And what would happen to you, Sue, as a child, if you showed any kind of weakness in your family?" Mia asks.

I wonder how that relates to how I am struggling, but I decide to trust this woman based on what Neda had said. What would happen if I showed any weaknesses? My mind instantly floods with images of memories. "Well, I remember a specific time when I was around six years old and we were living on a farm in South Florida. There was a particular horse my father had that I was deathly afraid of because it always acted so unpredictably. My father was the only one who could ride it. And then one day my father noticed I was afraid of it. So, he decided that was the day I was going to have to ride that horse no matter what. I remember crying, pleading with him, not to put me on that horse, but he did it anyway. As soon as he did, the horse took off with me crying hysterically on its back. I became so scared that I let go of the reins so I could hold on to the saddle horn with both my hands. The horse went into a full out gallop, heading directly toward a barbwire fence, and right before it looked like it was going to hit the fence, it slid its hind legs underneath itself and came to a sliding stop, arched its back, and threw me over its head into the barbwire fence. I was crying, trying to get the wire free from my hair and my face when my father arrived with the horse that had just thrown me off, and he plucked me out of the fence only to put me right back on that horse again until I learned not to fall off of it."

"I can feel how traumatic this felt to you. And so what did you decide about showing weaknesses?" Mia asks.

"That it's not safe to have them and you can never express them to others," I say.

"Because to have weaknesses means what, Sue?" Mia asks.

"That I am most likely going to die," I say, processing the words I was hearing myself say. I had never known I felt this way before and I was amazed and also perplexed at how I'd never seen this.

"Would it be accurate to say, Sue, that you have then been experiencing these kinds of feelings anytime you have to make a new decision? Like, any time you feel vulnerable, you feel anxious or concerned?" Mia asks.

I'm stunned hearing her words. I have never heard a clearer understanding for how I felt.

Mia checked in with me. "Does this make sense?"

I nod, and then realize I'm holding a phone. I say tearfully, "Yes! This makes total sense; in fact, it's probably the most sense I have felt in a long time." Mia goes on, "Although you don't need my permission, I do want you to know that you are in a completely safe space so feel free to allow your tears to release whatever naturally comes up for you."

"Thank you," I say whispering.

"When we have never been taught how to process our feelings, let alone where our feelings are actually coming from, and then we have experiences where our trust is broken, we experience an emotional trauma. And then what happens is that we decide it's not okay to feel this way, so we begin to suppress our true feelings, and act or pretend like we don't have any weaknesses. The irony is that by doing this, it only causes us to emotionally struggle more, which leaves us feeling like there is something wrong with us. Does that make sense, Sue?" Mia asks.

"I 've never understood this more clearly than I do in this moment," I say.

"*This is why if we don't heal the emotional side of ourselves, we actually limit our intellect,*" she says.

"Why?" I ask, becoming fascinated by what I am hearing.

"Because all behaviors are emotional, Sue; they are not intellectual. And by ignoring your weaknesses and not really dealing with them, they end up becoming some of your biggest blind spots that are causing you to feel stuck, stopped, and struggling, never having you experience yourself from your full potential. Unless..."

"Unless what?" I ask eagerly.

"Unless you awaken yourself to the Truth that is already in you," she says. "So, the first question I have for you, Sue, is are you ready to become *more* of who you really are?"

"Yes!" I say, more sure of it than at any other time in my life. I exhale deeply.

"Good," Mia says. "Are you feeling scared or even terrified right now?"

"Yes," I say.

"Good! Then we are on the right track. The second question I have for you, and sometimes this is the hardest one. Are you willing to stay the course? There is one key thing that everyone I work with must decide they will do, and it's called 'demonstrated consistency.' This means that although you will see immediate results, you must be willing to commit to consistently taking action with what, at first, will feel unfamiliar to you, before it will become familiar, and this is a daily commitment on your part. You will be supported, but I cannot do this for you, as success is an inside job before it becomes an outside reality. Is that clear?" Mia asks.

I feel a twinge of anxiousness, having heard Neda share the exact same thing. "But how will I do this?"

"You won't know how first, Sue. Your work is to decide to do it before you will know how. Consider your insurance company; did you know everything about how you were going to be successful first, before you decided?" Mia asks.

"No, I decided, and then I figured it out," I say, reflecting back on my life.

"Exactly, Sue, so the real question is, are you willing to give up that you don't know how? Are you willing to suspend your need to control long enough to decide, and then learn how?"

I cannot believe how much this woman can see right through me. And as terrifying as it feels to give up control, I feel an even bigger desire to learn how she is doing this. "Yes, I don't know how but I am agreeing. I'm ready."

"Great! Let's meet tomorrow at Café Susu, located at 240A Newbury Street at 5:00 p.m. Does that work for you?"

I check my calendar and add the appointment in my phone. "Yes, that works. I'll see you there!"

As I hang up the phone, I feel an excitement and elation in my body that I haven't felt in a very long time.

CHAPTER 3

THERE IS NO WAY TO AVOID RISK

"Wherever you are is the entry point."
– KABIR

At 5:00 p.m. sharp, I walk into Suit Supply looking for Café Susu. Then I see two men coming from the steps below with coffee. I follow the steps, and there below is a trendy, quaint-looking coffee bar. It is an eclectic mix between a European coffee bar mixed with a posh looking cigar bar, although there is no cigar smoking allowed. To add to the ambiance, I can sit and watch the women who are working there behind the glass, hemming and pressing away, preparing men's suits.

I walk over to the bar. "This is the coolest coffee bar I have ever been in!" I say as the beautiful blonde woman turns around behind the bar.

"Thank you! I am Julija." She reaches out to shake my hand. "I am the general manager and I am happy to hear you like it! May I offer you something to drink? We have the most amazing European coffees, champagne, or even some liquors."

"Sure, I would love a latte. Thank you!"

"Absolutely!" Julija smiles as she begins to make it.

When I turn around, something catches my eye. A pretty blonde woman is waving at me with a deep smile. I am surprised that Mia isn't as tall as I had imagined her. With a personality like hers, I thought she would be seven feet tall, when in reality she is petite and cannot be more than five-foot-four. I immediately wave back and go to greet her.

"Hi, I'm Sue," I say, extending my right hand in order to shake hers.

"Hi, Sue! Would it be okay if I hugged you instead? I am a hugger."

"Oh, sure!" I say. "A woman after my own heart."

"Please, Sue, let's sit," she says as she pulls out my chair. In that moment, Julija brings over my latte and takes Mia's order.

I suddenly start to feel nervous and more anxious than I expected. I take a sip of my latte.

Mia instantly notices and asks, "How are you feeling?"

"Nervous," I say, feeling embarrassed.

"That is completely normal as anytime we decide to do something different; our brain is going to warn us automatically in case of any impending danger. That's just your amygdala doing its job. Rather than you reacting to it, and reacting to your doubt, real power comes from when you pull back like a fly up on the wall observing down on the situation. In other words, become more present."

"Oh, ok," I say, pulling back and looking down at this situation.

"Now, ask yourself: is your life in any danger right now? In reality?"

"No," I say, feeling myself from outside the situation, and then feeling a bit silly for my nervousness.

"Good, now continuing to stay outside of this situation, ask yourself, what are the risks in doing this work?"

"Hmm... I guess the real risk is that I might be different. Right?" I say.

"And if you would be different, why is that a risk?" Mia asks.

"Because some people in my life may not like me?" I say, surprised by my own answer, as I had never seen that before.

"Good, Sue, and now, still staying outside of this situation, ask yourself this: what are the hidden risks, the ones you can't see, if you *don't* do this work? Meaning, if you don't do this work what does this really cost you? Because the Truth is that there is no way to avoid risk because there is always something that is at stake. Staying stagnant, in itself, has huge risks. Doesn't it, Sue?"

I exhale deeply. "*Yes!* It sure does. I guess I've never thought about it that way."

"The Truth is, as a human being, your birth automatically

puts you at risk of dying. And in case you haven't noticed..." Mia leans in, as if she is going to tell me a secret, smiling. "No one ever gets out of here alive."

I laugh, almost spitting up my latte.

"So, what's the Truth you haven't accepted about yourself?" Mia says.

"Hmm... I guess the fact that I am really going to die." I hear the naivety of my own words and wonder what reason did I have to feel afraid all these years? If I know I am going to die then everything seemed so foolish to me, in this moment.

"The truth is we can only ever decide which risks we'll take, and the greater the risk the greater the reward. So, the Truth is, Sue, for you to get the most out of your life, you will have to take more risks. And when you learn to risk in a way that unmasks the Truth, meaning you develop the ability to be fully present with reality, the risks you'll take will pay off with huge rewards. As the Truth will always set us free and it's our misunderstandings or misconceptions that will always keep us in bondage. Either way, you get to choose." Mia smiles.

I can feel the Truth in what she is saying as it resonates throughout my whole body.

"The biggest obstacle I see is not with people overcoming these doubts but that they never really challenged them. Is there something more specific you are nervous about?" Mia asks.

I think for a moment. "Can I really do this? I mean I have been this way my whole life, what if it is just too late for me? I mean, I've done a lot of personal development work, and I've gone to years of therapy, I am an avid reader, so I am aware of a lot of things, but I am also aware that the more I know, the more I still don't know. So I feel really frustrated that after all this work I've done in my life, I am *still* not where I want to be."

"Great, Sue, then let's clear that up, and clear what 'this' is versus what 'this' isn't," Mia says. "*In Truth, this is not about you doing more, as it is about you being MORE. Being MORE of who you really are. This is not about time, but rather a space from which you operate* as one of the biggest misunderstanding or misconceptions that people have is that it took them years to be the person they currently are. As if the way they are being is a *fixed way or a place they are at in life versus a space from which they are operating.*[3]

"This comes from a misconception or misunderstanding in our childhood where we are often taught that the future is some place to get to, like a place we are going to arrive. And the past is something that happened and is now over. Is that the way you have it? Is that what you've been taught, Sue?"

"Yes," I say. "But hasn't everyone?"

"Yes. But the Truth is linear time is actually an illusion. It's made up. It's a human construct. When in reality, what's happening is when you think of these moments what you are actually doing is experiencing them as if they are really happening, Now, as a present moment.[4] So anytime you are talking about a past moment, and you feel bad, what you are actually doing is keeping an obstacle between you and your success, because you are recreating the experience in your now. Does that make sense?" Mia asks.

"I think so. What you are saying is when I feel bad thinking back about an argument I had in my past with my now ex-husband, and I feel guilty for not having known better then, what I am actually doing is blocking my own success?" I ask.

"Yes, because anytime you are recalling, you're just using past images in your mind and then judging yourself, or others, for thinking that it should've been different or it shouldn't have happened. When in reality, it's not really happening, right now. So in a way, this is an attempt to justify or try to control a past moment that's not happening, but it will leave you experiencing that there is something wrong in your now."

"So, what's actually happening when I am worrying about my future?" I ask, curious about this new way of thinking.

"When you are worrying or concerned about your future, what you are actually doing is projecting images into your now of things you don't want, which is creating obstacles in the way of your success."

"Wow," I say, reflecting on how long I've been doing that.

"So consider, Sue, that all stress and unhappiness is happening when we are either trying to control a future moment or trying to control a past moment. Either way, it's not actually happening now, but it affects our now because 'now' is all that's happening in this present moment phenomena. And *our power, and therefore our potential, comes from us being fully present, moment by moment, by making accurate decisions in our now."*

Mia pulls a piece of paper out of her gold folder to show me this:

Now ⟶
(Present Moment)

⟵ Future
(Concerns or Worries)

⟵ Past
(Experiences or Memories)

Mia continues, *"This is also not about you trying harder,* or trying to better yourself, as that's all more of the same, of trying to control future and past experiences, and it is *exhausting."*

"Yes!" I said. "I am *exhausted!"*

"Yes! That *is* exhausting! Because trying harder is limited as it can only produce incremental gains. You are going against life, and that will eventually reach a point of diminishing returns, which will then leave you feeling burned-out. *This is also not about just reframing your thinking, or learning to memorize, or about trying to monitor, manage, or control your thoughts.*[5] *This is not just about getting more information but more about clearing the misconceptions or misunderstandings that are in the way of implementing your life's potential.* Look for yourself; how many people do you know who know a lot of information and yet they don't live the results they know?"

"Almost everyone, including me." I smirk.

"Yes, that's because you've been trying to change, fix, or improve yourself versus *awakening yourself to the Truth that is already within you by raising your conscious level of awareness and understanding on how life really works and how you can work with life.*"

Mia pulls another paper out of her gold folder:

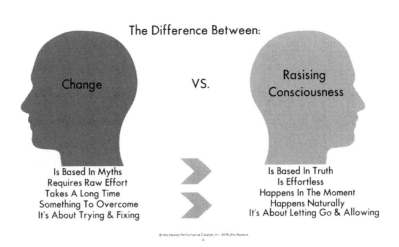

The Difference Between:

Change **VS.** Rasising Consciousness

Is Based In Myths	Is Based In Truth
Requires Raw Effort	Is Effortless
Takes A Long Time	Happens In The Moment
Something To Overcome	Happens Naturally
It's About Trying & Fixing	It's About Letting Go & Allowing

© Mia Hewett Performance Catalyst, Inc. All Rights Reserve

"See, here is the difference. Most people teach change, and while change is possible, just listen to any motivational speaker. It takes more effort and time than ninety-eight percent of people are willing to put in. And it is not because they are weak or necessarily lack willpower or drive. It's not because they are lazy, apathetic, or necessarily need more knowledge or passion! The reason ninety-eight percent of people 'fail' is because change is based in the myth that there is something wrong with you in the first place."

I sit there, absorbing this all like a sponge in water. I have a moment of excitement thinking about my future, and then quickly realize it isn't out there in the future. I become present again and feel in my body how wonderful it is to be here right now in this experience. I feel total love for this woman in front of me.

At that moment, Julija comes over with two glasses of water.

"May I get you ladies anything else right now?" she asks.

Mia looks at me as I shake my head.

"Thanks, Julija, we are good for right now." Mia smiles at her. As Julija leaves, she continues, "What this 'is' has more to do with you *consciously awakening*, which can be a lot like riding a bike. You see when you learned to ride a bike, all parts of you – your mind, your emotions, and your actions – had to come together in a harmonious way to ride the bike. Make sense?"

I nod.

"And the amazing thing is that once you *found where this feeling place is, inside of you, you forever shifted your consciousness on how to ride a bike*, because no matter how many years you may go without riding one, the moment you get back on a bike you automatically know exactly how to ride it. This happens in a moment, is effortless, and comes when you let go of your intellect to trust your innate intelligence, the feeling part of yourself that has you become one with the bike to carry you where you are aiming.[6]

"My Aligned Intelligence Method is exactly the same. Meaning once you debunk the myths you have and uncover your blind spots, understanding how to work with universal laws, and how to operate effectively and efficiently from your alignment by embodying who you really are, you'll forever shift your relationship with yourself, others, the world, your potential, your results, and therefore your success. *You change your world when you know how to shift reality.* And then your results will show up immediately as a reflection of this internal shift," Mia explains.

"Wow, Mia! This is incredible. Can it really be this easy?" I say, trying to get my head around everything she's saying.

"Yes, it's incredible, and profound, Sue, because it goes beyond the superficial symptoms to address the underlying cause, or core issue," Mia says. "*Life, is actually, meant for your success, and your work is to remove the obstacles that you have between you and this Truth. The fastest way for you to get from where you are to where you want to be takes three things.*

"*The first is* debunking the myths you have, by clearing up the misunderstandings or misconceptions that are keeping you stuck, stopped, and struggling, which are your blind spots.

"*Secondly*, it is in you knowing, understanding, and applying on purpose the Universal Laws of life. For when you work with these unseen forces rather than trying to control or push against them, you shift reality and create the results you do want in life. For it is law.

"*And thirdly*, it's going to take you learning how to function effectively and efficiently by operating from your own alignment. Meaning having all of your components, your mental, your emotional, and your physical, operating optimally, which *is* your full potential. *Real power comes from when what you think, what you say, how you feel, and what you are doing are* all *in alignment with what you want, instead of in opposition to what you want.* When we operate out of alignment, or are crosscurrent within ourselves, we cause mental, emotional, and physical breakdowns by having symptoms such as anxiety, depression, weight gain, or that of physical pain, or disease.   All are symptoms of a deeper root cause, which is the disallowance of ease within us. How does that sound?" Mia asks.

"It sounds amazing," I say, "and you make it all sound so simple."

Mia smiles. "Yes. And how you know what I am telling you is True, and that you can really trust it, is that it should be *simple. Wisdom will always take something that's complex and make it simple. But our intellect will always take something that's simple and make it complex.*"

"I've never thought about it that way," I say.

"Yes, because the knowledge we have is often coming from a misunderstanding or misconception that we have.

The key is to just start wherever you are, not where you would like to be. Meaning wherever you are in your conscious level of awareness and understanding *is* perfect, because it *is* where you are, and the only way to begin to shift reality is to first become present to where *you* are."

"Ok, so how do I shift my consciousness?" I say, eager to get started.

"I love your enthusiasm! For today, I want you to just take a step back and contemplate our conversation. Meaning for the rest of your day, check in by becoming present to what you are thinking. Notice whether you are in a future moment, worried about something that could happen, or if you are in a past moment upset about something that happened. Either way, pause, become really present by pulling back, and without any judgment, realize that the power you have *is* in the right now."

"Okay! I will do that," I say, overjoyed with this newfound power.

"Great work! Let's meet tomorrow, same time, same place."

CHAPTER 4

THE TRUTH ABOUT HOW LIFE ACTUALLY WORKS

"We don't see things as they are,
we see them as we are."
— ANAIS NIN

When I arrive at Café Susu, I find Mia already engaged in a conversation with Julija.

I walk up to the table where they are, and Julija immediately welcomes me.

"Good afternoon, Sue! Same order as yesterday?" Julija asks.

"Yes!" I say, excited to be here.

Mia smiles. "Are you ready for more?"

"I am." I say, sitting down and opening my notebook to begin.

"Awesome! Tell me, what has opened up since yesterday?" she asks.

"Wow, a lot." I shake my head. "I really got to see how much I am not in alignment."

"Great, Sue!" Mia smiles leaning toward me. "Tell me more."

"Well, I definitely got to see how many times I am not being present. Like when I become overwhelmed or confused. If I don't catch it right away, then I end up wanting to do something to avoid what I am feeling, like binge-watching my favorite show on TV." I smile.

"Fantastic awareness, Sue!" Mia says.

I smile back at her appreciatively. "And I also caught myself worrying about an upcoming event, wondering if I was going to do it right. Like if I was going to say the right things, and before, my mind would normally spiral out of control by becoming overwhelmed and confused, but this time I was able to pause, reflect, and just like you said, realize what I was thinking about and how that wasn't actually happening, and then I just let it go!"

"Oh, Sue! I am so happy for you!" Mia says.

"I really see that I've spent a lot of time not knowing that I wasn't being present in my life. And I can now also see just how detrimental this has been for me. As you said, the real cost, which I now see has been just how hard I've really been making all this."

"Yes. That's exactly right." Mia says. "The Truth is every living thing in this Universe was born to be a success because each living thing has within it the innate ability to be successful. Birds are born with the innate ability to fly, so they never have to go to flight school," Mia says smiling. "Squirrels, that are born in the spring, instinctively know how to gather nuts for the winter even though they have never experienced winter. *You were born being fully enough, more than capable having an inherent ability to create your dreams, and turn them into reality.*

"You see, you were born with an imagination as no one taught you how to imagine. Which gives you the ability to think intentionally by directing your thoughts. We call that visualization. You were born with feelings, as no one taught you how to feel, which is your own built-in internal GPS, that gives you the ability to know, at any moment, if the thoughts you are thinking are in alignment with what you are wanting, or if the thoughts you are thinking are out of alignment, with what you are wanting.

"And lastly, you were born with the ability to take action. Meaning you have the power to create your reality by visualizing clearly what you want, focusing on it intentionally, bringing out all the delightful details, knowing why you want it, and for what bigger purpose until it lives inside you as a new vibrational, emotional, set point. Then you have the ability to act in complete alignment by having full faith in doing what you would do if you knew you were going to succeed, behaving with absolute conviction. *In other words, your imagination, your feelings, and your actions are what give you the ability to create your reality.*

"So the question I have for you, Sue, is: *what's in your way of you seeing yourself as this success?*" Mia asks.

"Hmm... that's a great question." I say, never really having seen how much 'life' was for me.

Mia continues, "*The first biggest obstacle that stands in the way of most people is that they have never challenged their worldview.* Consider, if you were to ask a fish, how's the water? It would most likely say, 'What water?' Because we don't often see the water we swim in. Our worldview is just like water to a fish, as we've never thought to question the environment we live in. Specifically, we rarely challenge our existing beliefs or the conditioning that we were raised in. This is because these beliefs and conditioning already existed before we were ever born as they have always been present in the background of every conversation, yet most often, these conversations are filled with misconception or misunderstanding of how good or bad our parents feel about themselves. Most people are coming from their own background conversation inside their own moral framework of right and wrong.

"An example of this is how right or wrong the type of era they feel they, and therefore you, were born into. Whether they feel they are the right or the wrong kind of parent, or how right or wrong they feel about religion or nonreligious beliefs. The right or wrong they think about themselves, who they consider themselves to be or not to be, the right or wrong they feel about the kind of class they are or they aren't. The right or wrong they believe about relationships or the right or wrong they believe about the different roles that men and women are supposed to play. The right or wrong way they think about how to make money. The right or wrong way they have been taught about power, and whether they felt they had any or they didn't have any. The right or wrong they believe about sex and the human body, what was allowed and what was not allowed. The right or wrongs about their beliefs about food and weight. All of these rights and wrongs were based on the worldview *they* were born into and their preconceived ideas, opinions, judgments and thoughts about themselves.

"So can you see how these misconceptions or misunderstandings can then prevent you from living your full potential, feeling confident in yourself, and believing you can achieve your dreams?" Mia asks.

"Yes, I can totally see it." I say, reflecting back on my life and feeling for what has been in the background all along. "Especially in the times when I got in trouble for doing something wrong."

Mia smiled. "Which when you got in trouble, what kind of behaviors would that cause you then to do to avoid ever getting in trouble again, Sue?"

"I would start to try and please everyone."

"And do you notice that each person has different things they believe is the right way or the wrong way to please them, to do something?" Mia asks.

"Oh, yes; my mother's beliefs were different than my father's beliefs and my sisters' beliefs were different from our parents' beliefs. So I always felt like I had to be all these different kinds of people, in order to do things the 'right way,' which left me feeling like I was always doing it wrong." I say, feeling so good to say this out loud.

"Yes, and when you live with this misunderstanding or misconception, that satisfying everyone else's beliefs is your responsibility and you never question whether that is True or not, or whether those beliefs are what you are choosing, can you see *why most people believe their life is 'just the way life is'?*" Mia asks.

"Yes," I say, wow, I think, looking at the irony of it all now.

"*Life then feels like something that's done to you, or happening to you, instead of something that you can freely choose.*[7]

"*The Truth is to live your potential and feel confident in your power, you have to learn to be an independent thinker, using your internal intelligence, to discover what's True.* So the question I have for you is *who would you be without your worldview?*" Mia asks.

"Hmm... I don't think I even know?" I say.

"Great, as that's the best place to start: nothingness. Consider, most people aren't aware of the worldview they grew up in or the decisions they've made that are based on who they think they should or shouldn't be. All while trying to survive and gain the approval and acceptance of their parents and later their peers. Even those who chose to do the opposite of what their parents told them they should do, most often operate from making decisions based on proving others wrong, rather than truly living in alignment with what they desire. It's from these subconscious survival decisions and our worldview that we then form our beliefs, our ideologies, our attitudes, our judgments, and our personality which *all* then make up our perception of reality, or the way we see life."

Mia shows me an image from inside her folder:

"The illusion is we think our perception of reality is *all there is.* When in reality, everyone is experiencing their own perception of reality. For we don't see things as they are, we see things as we are. For example, imagine you are in a large house with many rooms and you are in the kitchen, someone else is in the bathroom, and someone else is in a bedroom, but everyone is in the same house. So the house represents the present moment reality and the different rooms represent each individual's unique perception of reality. So each of us is only aware of what we believe, based on our worldview along with the meanings we gave to our individual experiences, *which is now the keyhole that we try to live our life through,* called our perception of reality.

"This is why two people can grow up in the same household with the same set of parents and if you were to ask each one of them how was their childhood, each of them will give you two completely different stories." Mia says.

"Ha! Yes, I have had that exact experience with all of my sisters. It's funny how that happens." I smile.

"*The key is in understanding that each of us is having our own private experience that feels real to us, and yet the misunderstanding or misconception is that we think our experience includes all of reality in that moment.* How many times have you thought that something was really real, like the way you saw it was really how it was, only to find out later that it was a mistake in your perception?"[8]

"Many times!" I say.

"*The second biggest obstacle that stands in the way of most people is that they have been taught to believe that life works from the outside-in. When in Truth, life can only work from the inside-out.* Look around this café right now... notice that everything you see with your physical eyes was first imagined in someone's mind, held by an emotional feeling as a vibrational set point, and then followed all the way through by taking consistent actions, until it was created in reality. Nothing is happening from the outside-in. Nothing," Mia says, showing me a picture.

How We See Life:

I am separate from everything
I am connected to everything

VS.

I am Alone
I am Different
I am Misunderstood
I am my Perception

We are all Interdependent
I am a Part of it all
I am relatable
I am crafted with Intelligence of the Entire Universe

"When it comes to how you've been operating, what do you see?"

"I have definitely been living as if I am separate, like I am all alone, and no one really gets me. When my parents divorced and we moved back to the United States, I grew up poor, and so I always believed wealthy people were separate from me." Having said that out loud, a light bulb turns on in my head. "Oh, wow, I just realized that's why, even when I became wealthy, I never really felt wealthy!" I am amazed by this realization.

"Great awareness!"

"Hmm, wow! And I was always taught never to ask for anything, so I can see now why I always felt bad or guilty anytime I wanted something because deep down inside, I felt it was wrong for me to ask, and therefore even more wrong for me to have it. So even though I had money, I never felt wealthy as I never felt right about spending money on things that I desired for myself. I can also see how this added to me holding myself separate from everyone," I say, feeling a huge sigh of relief.

"And if life *really* works from the inside-out, what's the biggest misunderstanding or misconception you've been operating out of, Sue?" Mia asks.

"The illusion of separateness, my own perception of reality," I say, seeing it so clearly now.

"Yes," Mia says. "*Our belief in separateness is one of the biggest causes for us not living our true potential, as it keeps us from being in our power, present in every moment to achieve our dreams.*

"This is because when we have a belief that we are separate we actually resist or push against others and life, rather than finding how we could be capable by responding and connecting with others and life. *In Truth, everything is interconnected.*

"For example, the only reason we are alive right now is because of the trees that are giving us oxygen. We are so interconnected that we are often unaware of how they are constantly removing the poisonous carbon dioxide we are breathing out into our atmosphere. Through their photosynthesis process, they are returning to us the very oxygen we need to breathe.

So can you see that by holding life separate from who you are, you have no power then to live your potential?" Mia asks.

"Yes. I can see that," I say.

"*This is because our results will never exceed our expectations.*[9]

"*To shift our results, we have to shift our expectations. To shift our expectations means we have to be able to shift how we see life, or our perception of reality. We can only shift our perception of reality by becoming present with reality. The key being that life can only work for us when we work with life.*[10]

"When we hold ourselves apart from life, then we have no power to create something different. Does that make sense, Sue?" Mia asks.

"Yes, I am starting to see how blind I've been," I say.

Mia smiles, "*The third biggest obstacle that stands in the way of most people is that they are not aware that they are living in an all-inclusive Universe. Meaning, that most people believe their success is somewhere outside of them, a place to get to or something that just happens to the right people, something outside of their control, or something that is preordained based on God's will.* What's been your perception of how life and success work, Sue?" Mia asks.

"I'd have to say it always felt like it was something outside of my control. Like somehow if I could just get it right, or if maybe I could just do it right, or if I just take enough action then I might be able to have it." I sigh.

"Yes, and if life is outside of your control, what would be your go to pattern to try and make things work?" Mia asks.

"I would definitely resist people or try to find ways to control them, but mostly I would just try to avoid them for as long as possible. You know like that feeling of having toilet paper stuck to your shoe?" I laugh.

"Ah! Yes." Mia laughs.

"And then when I had reached my limit and couldn't take it anymore, then I would just go Tarantino on people and just kill everyone off," I said, hating to admit the Truth about myself. "I have a long list of dead bodies that I've killed behind me, Ha! *The Walking Dead* has got nothing on me." I wink at Mia.

Mia laughed.

"I can also see, that I believed life was really hard and that I would have to struggle; no matter how good I had it, I would always have to struggle," I say.

"Great awareness, Sue! Would you agree, based on those beliefs you had, that your life has matched exactly what you believed?" Mia asks.

"100 percent, I can see that," I say.

"Great! And what else are you now seeing about life?" Mia asks.

"I can see that I used to believe it was unfair, but now, based on what you are showing me, I see that nothing has been happening randomly, has it?"

"No. It's not. But if you've never been taught how life actually works and how to create it intentionally, then you end up creating it, by default, unintentionally," Mia says.

"That explains a lot!" I say.

"I'd like you to consider that God, or the energy force behind all that is, is already within you, and lives as innate infinite intelligence. Your acknowledgment and acceptance is what allows you to use this power to create the successes you desire. To become aware of this innate power and use your full potential you will want to first become aware the Universal Law of Cause and Effect."

Mia then shows me another photo.

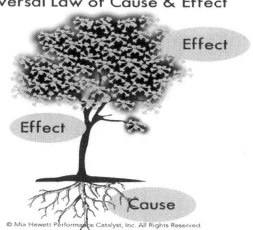

Universal Law of Cause & Effect

© Mia Hewett Performance Catalyst, Inc. All Rights Reserved

"The Truth is in an all-inclusive universe there is no such thing as no. Meaning the universe is always saying yes to whatever you are thinking, feeling, and believing whether it's positive or negative, it exists, and that's why what you resist always persists because everything is energy.

"The Universal Law of Cause and Effect states that nothing is happening by chance. For every effect there is a definite cause, and likewise for every cause, there is a definite effect. Meaning for every action, there is an equal and opposite reaction or consequence. Have you ever heard of this before?"

"Yes, in other words what you are talking about is 'we reap what we have sown,' right?" I ask.

"Yes, basically what this means is your thoughts, behaviors, and actions create specific effects that manifest and create your life as you know it. The key understanding in this is that this is an equal opportunity law. Meaning, it knows no difference between that which you say you want or that which you say you don't want. Because whatever you think about, and therefore internalize, will become the effects of that cause, as this is law. And this law is not based in morality.

"So, everything is technically created twice. Once internally in your mind, and emotions, and then acted on with a demonstrated consistency until it becomes realized in reality, externally. Does this make sense?"

"Yes, I am starting to see how this is all connecting." I say, excited and feeling empowered.

"Great, the second Universal Law that is important for you to become aware of and understand is the Universal Law of Polarity. This law says that nowhere in this universe exists a half of something. Meaning everything exists in an equal and opposite whole.

Universal Law of Polarity

"This means for cold to exist, hot must equally exist. For up to exist then down must also equally exist, for abundance to exist then the lack of abundance must also equally exist, at the same moment and time. For a problem to exist, then the solution must equally exist in the same moment and time. Not a different moment, as all of it is experienced in present moments, in the now.

"So if you are free to choose anything you want, what belief would support you in living your highest potential? Mia asks.

"The belief that I can live True to myself," I say, feeling strong in my decision.

"And to believe that, what would you have to give up thinking and doing?" Mia asks.

"Hmm, I would have to give up worrying and trying to please everyone. Like being worried about what other people are going to think about of me, and doing what everyone else says is the right thing to do instead of what would work best for me," I say, feeling proud of how clearly I am starting to see this.

"Awesome! The Truth about life, Sue, is it only works when we do," Mia says.

"These two laws are what will allow you your greatest power as they give you access to your ability to choose. *When you are choosing to consciously, and deliberately, create your life on purpose, then you shift reality and create the life you desire. It is law*," Mia says. "You become a force."

"Yes! This is what I have always wanted!"

"Wonderful! Let's meet tomorrow, same time." Mia grabs her gold folder putting it in her purse, and with a big hug, she waves, and is out the door.

"Isn't she amazing?" I hear Julija say as she's gathering our leftover coffee mugs.

"Yes, yes, she *really* is!" I say, smiling enthusiastically.

I look around the café, noticing it is still buzzing with energy, yet something feels different. Or maybe I am the one who's different. I smile at myself reaching down grabbing my belongings, enjoying this new sensation that is starting to become familiar throughout my whole body. I feel lighter and younger than I have in years.... Yes, life *is* genuinely exciting.

CHAPTER 5

HOW YOU CREATED YOUR OWN GLASS CEILING

"The degree to which a person can grow is directly proportional to the amount of truth he can accept about himself without running away."
– LELAND VAL VAN DE WALL

I am deep in thought, reflecting on all that has been transpiring in the last forty-eight hours and I realize just how much better I am feeling. I also feel a mix of emotions like those of guilt and remorse for somehow not already having known all this.

I feel guilty for divorcing my husband and breaking up our family because I didn't feel understood, I didn't feel important, and now I could see how I had contributed to my own suffering. I could see how each of us was living inside of our own worldview, our own perception of reality, and how neither one of us had the ability to see outside of what we had always known to find the Truth of what was causing our disagreements. I can also see how this left me feeling like it was all happening to me rather than seeing that my worldview and perception were all playing a part in it, so in that way I was choosing it whether I was aware of it or not.

And then there is another part of me that feels a tremendous amount of relief. Relief for all the years I'd felt like there was something wrong with me. Like I must be the crazy one! Because when you hear that often enough, you can start to believe it.

I was starting to see that I am not alone in all this and that I'm really not that different. Which makes me realize how I've been using my thoughts of being different as a kind of badge of honor and a way that I've been justifying my position – my way to be right.

And then I hear my name: "Hi, Sue! How are you today?" Mia asks.

"I'm great!" I say. "I am starting to see how this jigsaw puzzle, called life; all fits together!"

"Awesome. It feels so good to have it all make sense, right?" Mia winks at me.

"It sure does!" I say.

"Good!" Mia says, while pulling out the chair that's across from me and sitting down. "It's going to make even more sense after today! As we are going to continue to debunk the myths you have, clear up your misunderstandings or misconceptions, by going even deeper to uncover the specific obstacles that are keeping you from living your potential and being your power. *The fastest way for you to get from where you are to where you want to be is to realize where are you consistently going out of alignment.* Because wherever and whenever you are going out of alignment is where you have a rule or a glass ceiling."

"You mean like where am I self-sabotaging, right? And I don't even know that I am doing it?" I ask.

"Yes, whenever you are self-sabotaging you are hitting up against an internal wall, a glass ceiling, or a rule you've built that is most often unconscious to you. *In Truth, there is no such thing as problems. Because for a problem to exist the equal and opposite solution must also exist. So, there can only be two reasons why you are struggling. The first is because you have the wrong problem.* Meaning you think you know what the problem is, when in fact you have a misunderstanding or misconception that is hidden from your view, a blind spot. So, you are trying to solve the wrong problem, hence the reason why you struggle.

"*The second reason is that once you know what the right problem is, the only reason you would continue to struggle is that you haven't decided to solve it.* You see, to break through any glass ceiling, wall or rule you must first become aware of what the real problem is, and then you must decide to solve it by making it a priority. Because we really only make a priority that which we've decided to resolve. Make sense?" Mia asks.

"It does," I say.

"That said, there are three common patterns that all entrepreneurs struggle with that are stopping them from living their full potential.

"The first one is their need for approval."

"Yes, I definitely can see where I do this." I say.

Mia continues, "This comes from when we are children. Even if you feel that you've had the best parents, or that your parents had the best of intentions. When your parents have their own blind spots and myths about life, then they think you're not enough. They don't realize that you have your own set of intentions and longings, and then they themselves don't feel enough, but fear their own failures and shortcomings. They end up projecting their perception of reality onto you and then think it's their job to teach you how to be perfect, which is the biggest thing they fear they are not. And when you are not perfect, then they usually do what their parents did to them, which is to punish or shame you in some way by trying to make you feel guilty by telling you how wrong or bad you are. They go about withholding their love, connection, food, and sometimes, all three.

"So can you see why in the todays of your life, you can still have a misunderstanding or misconception about gaining someone's approval?"

"Yes, because somehow I think their approval will make me feel safe," I say, realizing this juxtaposition.

"Yes, because as children we didn't realize that our parents were actually having their own journey of self-discovery. As children we think our parents are *God*. And that's a misunderstanding or misconception in and of itself. Because in reality, would you die today if you did not get their approval?" Mia asks.

"No," I say.

"And so, can you see that it's our misunderstanding or misconception that when we feel we need our parents' approval that it is in this belief that actually keeps us creating our fear of people's judgments as adults?"

"Yes, I can see that."

"Because in Truth, can anyone ever really approve of you? I mean, where does approval come from?"

"From inside, right?" I say.

"Yes! So the misunderstanding that's keeping you needing their approval is that you are trying to solve an inside problem using an outside solution. And we can never do that. Because you could never meet enough people's approval to solve this problem for it is the wrong problem. Because the deeper problem is you don't believe you're capable of being enough."

I sit there, absorbing her words, realizing the Truth in what she is saying and amazed at just how widespread this misunderstanding *is*.

"To live your full potential, you must be willing to give up that someone outside of you has a greater authority over your life. That somehow others know more, or know better than you do. Does that make sense?"

"Yes," I say. "I feel like I would have to really be able to absorb this though in different situations, and with different people, to really feel like I know this."

"One hundred percent! *The second* most common pattern that all entrepreneurs struggle with that stops them from being their full potential is the role they've played in their family. As a child, Sue, whose judgment were you most afraid of? Your mother's or your father's?"

"My father's, for sure," I say.

"And so, what role did you play in your family to survive your father?" Mia asks.

I sit in silence, not realizing I had played a role. "I definitely felt like I had to try and please him."

"Yes, and if pleasing didn't work, what other roles would you take on? For example, did you become a comedian, a rebel, the black sheep, or were you someone who always got hurt, had something happen to you, so maybe you played the victim to deflect his judgment?"

"Yes, I can definitely see where I would play the victim any time I felt scared, like the situation was getting too heated or felt like it might get out of control, then somehow I would always end up getting hurt. And I can see now how that would defuse the situation by diverting everyone's attention from what was happening, onto me. The interesting thing is I don't ever really remember consciously deciding to do that. I just did it anytime I got scared," I say. "I just thought that's who I was, a clumsy person that always got hurt."

"That makes total sense, because prior to the age of about seven, we as humans don't have a conscious mind, we only have a subconscious mind, which is also known as our feeling mind. The reason this is important is without you having a conscious mind, you didn't have the ability to reject or accept an idea.   That means whatever someone told you, you believed as Truth, even when it wasn't. And you still believe it as it still exists in your programming today, until you evolve it."

"Wow," I say nodding my head, acknowledging her words.

Mia continues, "What other labels or roles did you become to survive? Were you the smart one? The gifted one? Or did you become the hero?"

"No, that would've been my older sister."

"If those were already taken, what role did you take on that you felt you could win at?"

"I feel like I took on the role of the mediator of my family. Because anytime anyone in my family was at odds with another family member, I felt it was my job to keep the peace." For the first time I see this so clearly and how I carried this same role into my past marriage.
"I can also see that I've always been the one who pleases others or takes care of everyone else," I say.

"Can you see that these roles, that at one time helped you to survive your life, are now part of the very pattern or problem, that's stopping you or hindering you from being the deliberate creator, thriving in your life?" Mia asks.

"Yes! I can see how these have held me back my whole life. As I've always felt like I was meant for so much more but I've struggled anytime I felt afraid that I am 'doing it wrong'.

I start doubting myself and then I question whether it's even worth it or not."

"Yes, because every time you are afraid of doing it wrong, do you notice that you stop being present with reality, and go right back to being a child who's trying to avoid —whose judgment?" Mia asks.

"My father's," I say.

"That's right." Mia adds.

"I feel like since I could never get his approval, and if I couldn't be perfect at something, then I didn't even want to try."

Hmm, "That's interesting." I say, hearing how ridiculous this sounds as my father has been deceased for many years now. "I can see that I've gone to great lengths to try not to fail, whether that's in my relationships, in my businesses, or with my money. I try to avoid anything that I don't feel I can win."

"Yes, most people who've been in your shoes, who have had the experiences you've had, who have linked pain to doing something wrong would, because your brain is designed to help you avoid pain and move toward pleasure. The problem is that if you are not aware that this is what's happening, that you have taught yourself to avoid discomfort, then the very thing that helped you to survive your life becomes why you aren't thriving in life.[11]

"*The third* most common pattern that all entrepreneurs struggle with that stops them from living their full potential is they have a desire for something but they have an underlying belief that's contradicting their desire. Which leads me to my next question for you: when did you decide you couldn't win at life?" Mia asks

"Hmm... I hadn't realized I'd made that decision," I say.

I look back at my childhood to see where that could've been. I start remembering all the many times that I used to win in life. Like when I was in the fourth grade, and the cutest boy had a crush on me, and then there was a dance competition for the entire fourth grade, and my crush asked me to be his partner, and we won! Amazingly, so did my two sisters and their partners. We each won our own grade.

Then I thought of the next event in my memory. It was when my mom, who used to be a P.E. coach, had hosted a ten-mile run for the entire school and I remember being really excited about it. So was my older sister. I remember my older sister, whom I had always shared a bedroom with, saying to me how big this run was to her. And then my mind takes me right back... it's a hot day, and the sun had been beating down on us for a while now. I am in fourth grade, and I am running. I can feel the dirt under my sneakers, and the sweat is dripping off my forehead. I am so thankful for the oranges they've been handing out, as they've been a small reprieve from the heat. I am on my last loop, and there are three of us in the lead. Michael, who is a year older than me is ahead of me, and my sister who is right behind me. Neither of us had ever run ten miles before. My heart feels both terrified and electrified like it is going to explode out of my chest from breathing so hard. I then feel a thrill of excitement the moment I realize I am going actually to win this! I am going to be the first girl who comes in! And in the very next moment, I also instantly realize just how upset and angry my sister is going to be if she lost, and I start to think about how alone I am going to feel, living in the same room. I slow down. She passes me and wins.

The emotional pain of my sister not liking me was far too great of a price.

"I decided it in the fourth grade," I say. "I just didn't realize I did it. I beat myself up pretty badly afterwards, and then I decided winning was just too emotionally painful."

"So, can you see that's why you avoid any moments that feel emotionally hard or challenging?"

"I can."

"So, what did you make winning mean?"

I think about her question and ask it to myself again, "I made it mean that for me to win someone else would have to lose and then they won't like me, or worse, they won't love me."

"Anytime you are in conflict within yourself, you will suffer Sue. Because your suffering is what's stopping you from achieving the results you desire most in life," Mia states.

"Why?" I ask.

"Because in a battle between your emotional beliefs and your logic, your emotional beliefs will win every time. That's until you evolve your beliefs to match your desires.

In other words, you can't go against yourself and thrive, as those are opposing beliefs. Notice, what you do to compensate whenever you feel an inner conflict? Where you have a desire for more, but a fear of winning?" Mia asks.

"I avoid certain situations, and hold myself back," I say.

"Yes, and where else are you settling in your life, Sue?"

"Everywhere! I say, "I play it safe by only having safe goals. Goals that don't really challenge me, or that I don't really care about, goals that I won't put a deadline on so that people can't judge me if I don't accomplish them." I see this so clearly for the first time. "This is also how I let myself off the hook because if I don't accomplish it, then I tend to justify it by telling myself that it wasn't really that important or worth it anyway."

"Yes. Can you see that *if you are going to be True to yourself and live your highest potential, you must be willing to give up the roles* that *you've been playing, give up needing other people's approval, and give up your habit of saying you want something and then believing the opposite*?"

"Yes, I can see how I am doing all of that!" I say.

"*To think thoughts based on what you were taught is easy. To think Truth, regardless of what you were taught takes effort, and it's the most important effort you could ever undertake.*

"The truth is, you were born for success but you've been conditioned and have decided to settle. Anytime you internally go against yourself, you create your own glass ceiling, your own upper limit, and therefore, your own struggle," Mia says.

"The great news is your beliefs are not fixed! Because beliefs are just habits of thought that you keep thinking. Have you ever noticed that some of the beliefs you had as a teenager are not the same beliefs you have in the todays of your life?" Mia asks.

I laugh. "Yes, and thank goodness!" I say.

Mia laughs too. "Just because you believed it, doesn't make it True, it just means you believed it. *Whether you want to create a belief on purpose or whether you've created a belief by default, it takes the exact same process.*

"*One: you first have to hold your focus on a thought or idea consistently enough that you internalize it by giving it a meaning.*

"*Two: you then have to feel it emotionally, in your gut, so that it becomes an internal emotional set point.*

"*Three: you then have to make this new feeling place so familiar that it becomes how you see yourself* so that every time you think the thought, you feel this feeling, you see yourself this way and that's how you'll believe it and how your idea will become a belief."

"I never realized this." I say, dumbfounded.

Mia smiles. "In a moment, I am going to ask you to close your eyes, and reflect inward as I ask you a series of questions, all while you ask yourself this one important question, 'Who am I?' Now close your eyes and ask yourself:

'Who am I?' Are you the worldview you were born into?" Mia asks.

"No," I say.

"Are you your perception of reality?"

"No," I say.

"Are you the roles you've played? Meaning, if you stopped playing those roles and start being another role, would you still be you?" Mia asks.

"Yes."

"So, are you the roles you've played?" Mia asks

"No."

"Are you your personal history?" Mia asks.

"Yes."

"Meaning, if you no longer have the same perception of your history, would you still be you?"

"Oh, yes," I say.

"Then are you your personal history?" Mia asks again.

"No," I say, realizing I'd still be me.

"Are you a label or an identity? Meaning, if you were no longer a business woman, would you still be you?" Mia asks.

"Yes." I say.

"So, are you the label of being a business woman?"

"No," I say.

"Are you what others have told you that you were? Meaning, are you your conditioned beliefs?"

"No," I say.

"Are you what you have? Meaning, if you stopped having what you have, would you still be you?"

"Yes," I say.

"So, are you what you have?"

"No," I say.

"Are you your attitude? Meaning, if you shifted your attitude and you took on a new one, would you still be you?" Mia asks.

"Yes," I say.

"So are you your attitudes?"

"No," I say.

"Are you the behaviors you do? Meaning, if you took on new behaviors, would you still be you?"

"Yes." I can see myself doing different behaviors and I would still be being me.

"So are you the behaviors you do? "Mia asks.

"No," I say.

"Are you the beliefs you have about yourself?"

"No." I say.

"Are you the thoughts you think?" Mia asks.

I pause and think about that.

Mia continues, "Meaning, if you shift your thoughts and have different thoughts, would you still be you?" Mia asks.

"Yes," I say.

"Then are you your thoughts?" Mia asks again.

"No," I say with this realization.

"Are you the emotions you feel? Meaning, if you shift your emotions, would you still be you?" Mia asks.

"Yes," I say.

"So, who are you?" Mia asks.

I sit in silence feeling an emptiness from all I've ever known... "Nothing," I say.

Mia let me sit with this for a few moments before continuing softly, "Exactly. Consider Sue that so much of who you think you've been has been nothing but an attachment to an illusion. And yet, every decision you have made has been coming from who you think you are."

I sat in silence, amazed by the magnitude of this one thought.

"Inside your nothingness consider that the essence of who you are is a force powered by an energy far greater than any conditioned worldview, than any role, than any label, than any identity or personality, than any behavior, and beyond any human conditioned belief. Meditate on this Sue, and I will see you tomorrow, but this time we are going to meet at my office."

"I never even knew you had an office," I say, having always met her at a café.

Mia laughs. "Yes! In the building where I live I have quite a few different offices at my disposal. I'll text you the address."

Mia gets up, smiles at me, gives me a warm hug and with that, she is out the door.

CHAPTER 6

THE INVISIBLE TRAP
YOU'VE BEEN STUCK IN
(WITHOUT EVEN KNOWING IT)

"We can't solve problems by using the same kind of
thinking we used when we created them."
— ALBERT EINSTEIN

"Hi! Welcome!" Mia says as she opens the huge front door to her building.

"Wow, this is spectacular!" I say in awe of her buildings modern interior. I am surprised that it even exists in Boston, which is more known for its historical properties.

"Thanks! In the todays of my life, I really enjoy having all of life's modern conveniences, like a gym, a pool, a media room, but none of the responsibilities of having to maintain them all. I've learned that life can be so much more with less." Mia winks at me. She then shows me into a private conference room that is surrounded by floor-to-ceiling glass where in the middle of the conference table is an assortment of fresh juices and fresh fruit, along with bottled water, an assortment of yogurts, and protein bars.

"Help yourself," she says.

I grab a bottle of water and a protein bar and then sit down.

"Have you seen the movie *Inception*?" Mia asks.

"Yes, I have. It's a great movie!" I say.

"Yes, it is! And today is going to make even more sense as you discover your own inception," Mia says, smiling with a bit of seriousness in her voice.

"Really?" I say, a bit shocked and curious at the same time.

"Do you remember when the main character that's played by Leonardo DiCaprio asks, what the most resilient parasite is? Bacteria? A virus? An intestinal worm? And then he says that it is an idea. Because once an idea has taken hold of the brain, it's almost impossible to eradicate," Mia says.

"Yes," I say. "Now that you say that, I remember it."

Mia continues, "And then, in the movie, his wife, who stored away an idea, that he had implanted in her mind, becomes lost in what's reality and what's her perception of reality."

"Ha! Yes," I say.

"Well, inception is a point whereby an idea is instilled into your mind, that you then believe to be True, and then this becomes your perception of reality, forgetting that you were the one who believed it." Mia pauses, letting me absorb what she is saying. "Consider that all of us have created our own inception, and have been lost in it, until we awaken to this Truth. *The number one obstacle that stands in people's way of being their full potential is they don't know who they are versus who they are not.* You see, until you know *who you are not*, consider, you don't really know *who you are.*" "As it is the contrast that allows you to see the difference. For example, you don't truly know cold until you know hot, you don't know your left until you know your right, and you don't know who you are until you know clearly who you are not. Does that make sense?" Mia asks

"Hmm, yes. I never saw it that way before, but I can see that if everything looked the same I wouldn't be able to tell the difference because I wouldn't be able to see the contrast."

"Exactly." Mia says staring into my soul. "Are you ready, Sue, to see who you aren't?"

"Yes, I am intrigued!" I say.

"Great," Mia says. "In a few minutes, I am going to ask you to take me back to a time, in your earliest memory, when you were really young when there was a harmony within you. Where you trusted yourself, you trusted others, and you trusted life, and then something happened. Something that can feel like it was no big deal now, but back when it happened, at the age you were, it was a *big* deal, as you had never had that kind of experience happen before, and emotionally you didn't feel like you were capable of being with the experience.

"The majority of the time this event happens before the age of seven and most often it's between the ages of two and four years old. Now, the great news is you don't have to try and figure this out, as your subconscious mind already knows. It's like the hard drive in your computer and your hard drive never forgets. All you have to do is just ask yourself, 'what's the earliest memory I have, when I felt like something happened that I didn't see coming, and I felt an immense amount of sadness or fear, or felt something must be really wrong with me?' For example, let me tell you about a client of mine, we'll call him Dave. When Dave first came to me it was because he had never had any real success. He consistently struggled to make money. As quickly as he would make some money he would just as easily lose it. When we started our work together he didn't really think he had anything traumatic happen to him. He told me he had a good childhood and had good parents. But after some deeper prompting he remembered something that happened when he was around four years old.

"He said, 'I don't think this could be it, because it really wasn't that big of a deal.' I told him to just trust himself and his subconscious mind, as it always knows. Then he remembered this one night: 'Well, I was around four years old, and my twin brother and I were sleeping in our bedroom, and out of a deep sleep I remember my mother waking us up in a tremendous panic! She was petrified and yelling, 'Get up, get up, hurry, hurry, hurry, get under my bed and don't come out until I tell you. Your father is coming home, and he's drunk! And I don't want him to hurt you.' I ran with my brother and we hid underneath her bed. I noticed my twin brother was not at all fazed by what was happening. He ended up falling quickly back to sleep. I, on the other hand, felt so terrified that I had no idea that my father could do something that could hurt me... I was so scared, I blacked out. I don't remember much of anything else that happened that night, but the next day I remember I would start crying easily. I became really emotional, and my family started to call me 'the sensitive' one. I also became the shy one, as I was always afraid that something bad might happen at any moment. Like I always had to watch over my shoulder for when the next shoe was going to drop.'

"As an adult, Dave's twin brother grew up and became the 'successful one,' the 'confident one' while Dave consistently struggled. Because just like a fish that doesn't see its own water, Dave never saw that this one experience was the inception that would go on to alter his future. A pattern that would go on to cost him a fortune and leave him feeling scared, confused and powerless as he never felt safe again until we cleared this pattern from his programming and his consciousness evolved.

"Within two months' time, Dave went on to quadruple his income, something that can appear miraculous to others, but in fact is something that can really be a commonplace occurrence.

"Can you see how one traumatic experience can affect every part of your life? From your relationship with yourself, how you see yourself? From your relationship with others, to your relationship with money or your relationship with your body, your health, or even the relationship you have with life itself?"

"Wow," I say, still deep in thought. "It's amazing that he didn't think this was a trauma."

"The key is understanding that all traumas are in the eye of the beholder, not in the situation."[12]

"The reason is, that when we think of a trauma, we most often think that it has to be something extreme, like we almost died or we were severely sexual abused, and while those experiences are definitely traumatic, so is growing up with a parent, or a sibling, that is continuously moody. The Truth is that anytime a child experiences an emotional loss of love and connection in which they no longer feel safe, they will experience an emotional Trauma.

"As John Bradshaw once powerfully said, '*Shame is the greatest form of learned domestic violence.*' And *the Truth is, any trauma left untangled will become a self-fulfilling trap!* A lot like a Chinese handcuff."

Mia grabs a picture out of her gold folder.

A Chinese Handcuff

Any trauma left untangled becomes a self-fulfilling trap.

"A Chinese handcuff?" I say.

"Yes, because just like a Chinese handcuff the more you try and resist or try to control it, the stronger the trap becomes. Therefore, the way out of a Chinese handcuff, or any unwanted emotional experience always feels counterintuitive. You have to be willing to let go of the control that has you trapped to then surrender and become' curious which will allow you to receive the clarity that sets you free.[13]

"The fastest way to get from where you are to where you want to be is first to discover who you really are versus who you are not.

"So now it is your turn. Take me back to a time, in your earliest memory, when you were really young when there was a harmony within you. Where you trusted yourself, you trusted others, and you trusted life, and then what happened?" Mia asks.

I think back in my mind, drawing a blank. I ask myself the question again, becoming curious about what it could be. At that moment, it felt like a small haze lifted and a particular memory started to flood my mind. I begin to remember something I'd forgotten a long, long time ago.

"I think I was around five years old... we used to live on a farm. I loved being outside with the animals because it's where I felt the most alive." I smile.

Mia smiles back at me.

"I mean each animal had its own personality! And I found them all to be so amusing in their own unique way.

Of course, I had a few favorites, for different reasons. Like there was my pig Sucia, and all her little piglets. She would become so protective of them! And then there was our amazing horse I loved, called Sunset. She was a beautiful chestnut mare, and I can still remember lying on her back, for what seemed like an eternity while she grazed in our pasture. With her, I was determined she could read my mind! I would say things to her like, 'If you can hear me, then wiggle your right ear' Or 'If you can hear me then swish your tail' And, of course, as soon as she'd move, I would convince myself it was because she had heard me." I laugh, reflecting on these fond memories.

"I am not even sure where I got that from, but I was convinced it was true because I used to watch how all the animals would communicate so often and without ever making a sound. So, I felt like there was this shared language among them and I wanted to be able to 'speak' it. I'd lay there on my horse's back, looking up at the clear blue sky, feeling a deep connection to her, and everything around me. And it was in those moments that I felt like I was a part of something so much bigger than myself, and life was beautiful." Then as soon as I said that, I instantly felt a deep sadness come over me when I realized that something I loved was missing.

"And then what happened was... I was sitting in my bedroom, and I heard my father calling me, but I didn't answer right away because I remember being busy! I was trying to comb out my favorite doll's hair." I smile at my pureness and the simplistic thinking I had as a child. "I remember feeling frustrated because I'd gotten her hair wet the night before, while I was taking a bath, so I was sitting there struggling to untangle her hair.

"And I heard him again. Only this time when he called out my name it was a lot firmer and louder, 'Sue Marie! Are you back there?' I knew he meant business as the implication was in his voice.

"So, I remember I jumped to my feet because I didn't want him to grab his belt. And as I came around the corner, I saw him standing there. I immediately started to search my brain for anything that I could've done wrong, but I couldn't think of anything. He told me to come outside. And I was like, 'Ok, but why?' I didn't understanding why he would be asking me and not all my other sisters.

"And then he said, 'I want you and I go spend some time together.' And I remember being in disbelief. I mean he usually would do something with my older sister, Ann, as she was his favorite. She was the tough one, the brave one, the boy he never had. But I followed him outside that day anyhow, feeling so special that he picked me.

"And as we walked toward the barn, he asked me, 'Which one of these is your favorite chicken?' So I yelled, 'That one!' and then he said, 'Good,' and without changing his tone, he said, 'That's the one we are going to kill today.'

"I remember being instantly shocked, not understanding what I'd just heard. My mind became scrambled with confusion. I started yelling and crying, trying to think about all the things I might say that would take back what I had just done. But it was too late. Within seconds he had grabbed her by the throat and reached for his machete and then instantly it was done. And I was devastated. It was all my fault!

"I remember he had made me pluck her while I wept. I became a vegetarian that day, deeply saddened by this whole experience, but what I am most angry about is that I never saw it coming," I say, crying, feeling full of guilt.

"I'm deeply sorry." Mia says with compassion. "You are doing an amazing job, Sue. I'd like you to take a few deep breaths."

So I did.

"And now, breathe, until you feel a sense calmness, feeling your feet back on the floor, bring yourself back into this room.

"*Next*, I want you to become an observer of this experience. Meaning, I want you to take me back through this experience, but this time as an observer, so I want you to pull back away from this experience as if you are a fly high up on the barn wall. You'll know when you are genuinely observing because you'll have the ability to thoroughly see this experience from a neutral perspective as if you are watching it on a movie screen.

"I want you to go back now and see it from outside yourself, hear what you heard, your father calling your name, listen to what your father says, see what you saw, your father is doing precisely what he did before, yet as the observer notice what you made this experience mean. What's the story you told yourself about this experience?" Mia asks.

"Hmm, I definitely decided it was all my fault. Like I can see from this view that I made it mean that if something this horrible could happen to my favorite chicken, that I didn't even know was possible, then obviously something awful could also happen to me. I can see where I decided that there must be something really, really, wrong with me because I never saw this coming." I say.

"Yes, because what did you make it mean that you never saw this coming?" Mia asks.

"That I must be a really horrible person. That I must not be smart, right? Because why would a smart person do this? I can also see where I made it mean that I am all alone in this world. That I am not important, because no one really cares what I saying, so what I have to say doesn't matter."

"You are doing great, Sue.

I want you to become aware that these meanings and judgments you said about yourself Is your Chinese handcuff. This is your emotional trauma that became your self-fulfilling trap. Can you see this is the day you decided that something must be wrong with you?" Mia asked.

"Yes, I said there must be something so wrong with me, that no one should ever know just how horrible of a person I really am," I say.

"Yes, because when we are children, Sue, and we experience an emotional trauma where we don't believe we are capable of being with an experience, we think who we *really* are must be flawed, like there is something wrong with us. And when those feelings become unbearable, we will then decide to hide this part of ourselves by cover it up –creating our Chinese handcuff, our self-fulfilling trap- Our Ego Identity.

"The next thing I want you to do is distinguish this experience by separating out your ego from the actual situation."

Mia pulls out a diagram titled "Who I Became to Survive."

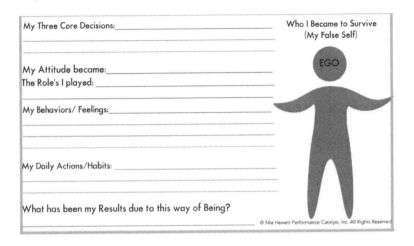

"As a result of this experience notice who you became to survive your life...what were the three core decisions you made about yourself, others, and the world, that day?" Mia asks.

"I decided I couldn't trust myself" I say, because I never saw it coming so I felt like I must not be smart, and I definitely couldn't trust others because they don't really mean what they say. And the world, hmm, is not how it appears, as it's not safe. I also decided that it's not safe to show people how you really feel, because when I show people the truth about how I feel, really awful things happen. I can also see that I decided that in order to be safe, I could never let anyone ever get too close again. I can't be vulnerable."

"Because what did you make being vulnerable mean?" Mia asks.

"It feels like being vulnerable means death," I say, realizing this for the first time.

"And as a result of making these core decisions, Sue — that you could not trust yourself because you're not smart, you can't trust others, as they don't mean what they say, and the world is not how it appears, as it is not safe, and to be vulnerable would be death — what then became your attitude to survive your life?" Mia asks.

"My attitude became one of complete mistrust and extreme cautiousness. I can see now how I became someone who is always silently worrying," I say.

"And so, as a result of that day when you decided that you couldn't trust yourself as you're not smart, and you can't trust others, as they don't mean what they say, and the world is not how it appears, as it's not safe, and to be vulnerable would be death, and your attitude became one of being a silent worrier who mistrusts and is extremely cautious. What then became your new behaviors and feelings?" Mia asks.

"I became a quiet, shy kid, who only expressed her emotions when I was alone, or when I thought no one was looking." I say, remembering a time when my mother, who gave me a pair of English riding boots for Christmas, found me in our garage, alone, jumping up and down with excitement, in complete silence. "I can now see that the world changed that day for me from being a bright, sunny, happy, place to a dark, fearful, and alone one."

"Yes, and so as a result of that day when you decided you could not trust yourself, as you are not smart, and you can't trust others, because they don't mean what they say, and the world is not how it appears, as it is not safe, and to be vulnerable would be death, and your attitude became one of being a silent worrier who mistrusts people and is extreme cautious, and your behaviors and feelings became one of a quiet shy kid who went from feeling happy to feeling fearful and alone. What then became your behaviors or daily habits from this new way of thinking and being?" Mia asks.

Hearing Mia reflect this back to me, I realize something. "I became someone who has been trying not to be seen, trying not to stand out, to be as small as possible, to survive. I started trying to please everyone. I started being overly nice, not really being straight or direct with people, being someone who pretended that nothing bothered me, which then only made me feel even more alone, like no one ever really understood me, because no one ever really saw me or knew the Truth. I stopped sharing how I truly felt as I was afraid of being vulnerable and being made wrong." I say, feeling a tremendous amount of sadness come over me.

"You're doing amazing," Mia says. "Just allow these emotions to come up and freely release them as you're in a completely safe space.

As someone who's been trying not to be seen, trying not to stand out, and trying to be as small as possible, pleasing everyone by being overly nice, and not really being straight with people but pretending that nothing is really bothering you, leaving you then feeling even more alone, like no one understands you, trying to survive your life, what results do those behaviors then create in your life?" Mia asks.

"Definitely not the results I want!" I say, laughing at the obvious.

"Exactly. So can you see, Sue, that as a result of this one emotional experience, this trauma, this inception, when you decided that you couldn't trust yourself, where you made the decisions that you're not smart, and you can't trust others, and the world is not safe, and to be vulnerable would mean death, so you could never let anyone ever get too close to you, can you see that these core decisions then became your attitude, your behaviors and feelings, your way of being or operating, that has then gone on to create the results you've been getting in your life?" Mia asks.

I had never had my life expressed this succinctly before. "Wow. Yes. When you say it that way, I can see how my whole life has been summed up through this one experience," I say, amazed at how this changed the way I saw everything.

"Now this time let's clear up the misunderstandings or misconceptions that have been keeping you stuck, stopped, and struggling in this self-fulfilling trap. Observe the experience again, but this time I want you to separate the Truths from the Lies that you told yourself.

What were the lies or the self-judgments you told yourself about this experience?" Mia asks.

"Hmm, well I can see that I told myself a lie that I couldn't trust myself," I say.

"Yes, and why is that a lie?" Mia asks.

"Well because I can trust myself, as I knew there was something off in my father that day. I just couldn't put my finger on it." I say, feeling my sense of power returning.

"Awesome. What other lie do you now see?" Mia asks.

I thought about her question. "My whole life I've always thought of myself as a confused person, but I am starting to see now that I don't have to be confused. That my confusion is actually another lie," I say, feeling my confidence returning.

"Yes. Consider that your confusion only happened because you didn't think you were capable of being with this experience. And why is that now a lie?" Mia asks.

"Because I am capable of being with it, I just didn't know how." I say.

"Exactly, so can you see the misunderstanding you had as a young child was you thought you had to know how first, before you could be capable, when the Truth is you just have to decide you are capable, then the how will show itself. " Mia says.

"Yes, I can see that now." I say.

"Fantastic. What other lie do you now see?" Mia asks.

"The lie that I can't trust people." I say.

"And why is that a lie?" Mia asks.

"Because my mother has always done what she said she was going to do. So it is simply not true that I can't trust all people." I say.

"And what do you think is the lie Sue, in the decision that vulnerability means death?" Mia asks.

I laugh out loud hearing Mia say this seeing this experience now a bit more comical. "I can see how I exaggerated that just a wee bit as I clearly was vulnerable in this experience. And I did not die." I say, laughing

"Yes, and lastly, what's the lie in your decision that the whole world is not safe?" Mia asks, smiling.

"Well, that's clearly a lie!" I say, laughing at myself. "Hmm, I put the whole world into my experience!" I say.

"Yes, consider, Sue, that day you put the whole world into a keyhole based on your perception of reality when in reality do you think there were a lot of other great experiences that were happening in the world in that exact moment?" Mia asks.

"*Yes.* I am sure there were," I say.

When you observe this experience and see the difference between all of reality *that was happening at that moment versus your perception of reality or what you made your reality mean, you awaken to the Truth*. Because in Truth, knowing what you know now, that life is created from the inside-out, not the outside-in, who did you really betray in that moment?" Mia asks.

"Myself," I say.

"Yes, and for you to live your full potential and create the life you want, you must be willing to forgive yourself. Meaning you must be willing to be forgiving to yourself to see the gift in this experience because *the Truth is to transcend the trap, you must be willing to let go of it.* So, Sue, are you ready to forgive yourself?" Mia asks.

"Yes," I say, feeling the power of my decision.

"Great, because when you can see the difference between your ego and reality, you awaken. And to do so requires that you be willing to look, without any preconceptions, of how you thought it should or shouldn't have happened, to see what you initially thought was evil to find the beauty in it.[14]

"Alright, you have done an amazing job Sue! Let this now integrate by just allowing yourself to be with your newfound Truth," Mia says.

"Thank you," I say as tears begin to flow down my cheeks as I am still processing all that had just transpired. "I am truly and eternally grateful as no words can describe the amount of gratitude that I am feeling right now. Thank you for helping me through this and being a guiding light."

"It's my pleasure," Mia says, smiling with compassion.

And with that, we schedule our next meeting, as she gives me clear instructions to begin taking action from having complete faith, trusting in my success, as it is my birthright. Mia hugs me as she escorts me out her front door leaving me to marinate on all that just transpired.

CHAPTER 7

THE SECRET TO BEING UNAPOLOGETICALLY YOU

"You are the Universe, you aren't in the Universe."
– ECKHART TOLLE

I wake up earlier than usual, realizing there is no light piercing through my bedroom blinds. I take a deep breath. I can't fall back to sleep as I feel a sort of giddiness inside. A sort of childlike wonder thinking about what I am going to discover today! Something I haven't felt in a very long time. And yet here I am, feeling anticipation and excitement knowing that something amazing is going to happen. Yes, I think to myself, there is definitely something different about me but what? The first thing I notice is how much I lighter I feel but why? I ask myself, and then I remember.

In my dream, I am back on my farm, and I am wearing a long, white pajama dress and I am playing in my backyard as I am looking for something in the bushes behind our house. I notice Sunset, my beautiful horse, watching me as I search the bushes looking for any critter I can find to play with. And then I see her, my favorite chicken Henny Penny! I am so excited; as she notices me, too, and begins running toward me. In all my happiness, I squat down opening my arms out wide, wanting to give her the biggest hug, but she's not interested in my embrace. She's looking to see if I have any worms for her. I laugh; she is precisely the same. So I dig in the dirt and find her a worm she willingly takes right out of my fingers. Then I hear my mother's voice calling, I smile, my heart filled with joy at Henny Penny and go inside.

As I am laying here awake now in my bed, I feel so grateful to have been able to see her, even if it was only in a dream. I feel a strong sense of appreciation for that part of my life, and acknowledging this, I immediately feel a kind of expansiveness open up inside me that wasn't there before.

I stretch, get up, and turn on the shower and as I begin to take off my clothes, I am struck by the symbolism of how it feels to strip away a lifetime of self-perceptions, self-imposed limitations, and self-imposed beliefs. As I shower, I allow the water to thoroughly cleanse my body, washing away with each drop a lifetime of unanswered questions, lost hope, and unrealized dreams, leaving in its presence a newness of renewed faith and trust.

As I step out of the shower, I am amazed at how refreshed I feel, mind, body, and spirit. I realize this has been the best shower I've ever taken. I dry off and put on my favorite blue shirt, slip on my favorite pair of skinny jeans, pull on my favorite pair of Juicy Couture riding boots, and I head out the door. Just like that, I am back at Tatte's coffee house, not exactly sure how I've even driven there. I feel like a star in my very own movie, like the world, overnight, had become my playground, created just for me to explore and I didn't want this to end. A light snow had fallen the night before bringing a newness and aliveness to everything I see.

I enter Tatte's coffee house and get in line. I notice right away that I am seeing everyone as if I am wearing a new pair of glasses.

"Your usual? A twelve-ounce latte with an extra shot, no foam?" Sara says without breaking a smile.

"Yes, Sara, but today make it two!" I say, smiling at her. This time I can see that Sara isn't actually present, that she is preoccupied, elsewhere, with something else on her mind.

When she returns with the lattes I say, "Thanks, Sara! Hey, I just want you to know I really appreciate you."

I can see she is a bit taken back.

"Oh," she says, "thank you." She hands me my two lattes, just in time for me to grab a couple seats from two people who are just leaving.

As I sit down, I notice a woman directly to the right of me who is scrolling through her social media feed, only slowing down to read the comments on a post, and then looking to see how many likes it has before deciding whether or not she's going to like it. I can feel her concern, that question of "Is it safe to comment or not?" I can even feel her deeper concern of what will people think of her if she does comment or likes the post.

Just then, I see another woman enter the café. She instantly notices I am looking at her and becomes concerned, as if I was looking at her because there must be something wrong. She quickly checks herself, brushing off anything that could be on her dress, just in case.

I then glance at the man sitting to my left and I can feel him become uneasy, he shifts his position, turning his back slightly toward me as he adjusts his newspaper.

"Good morning, Sue!" I hear Mia say.

"Good morning, Mia!" I say, as we exchange hugs.

"How are you?" Mia says. "Have you started experiencing things differently?"

"Yes!" I say with a slight laugh. "The world is different to me today. Or maybe it would be better to say that I am different in the world."

"Fantastic!" Mia says.

"I've been sitting here observing people just as they are and it's amazing to me how many people live in their concerns," I say reflectively.

"Yes," Mia says.

I continue, "And it has nothing to do with me as I am actually not at all judging them."

Mia's smile gets bigger and bigger.

"What?" I ask, wanting to know what she sees.

"I love seeing you get this!" Mia says.

I pick up my coffee and lean back confidently in my chair allowing her acknowledgment to really soak in. "Do you mean how clear everything has become?"

"Yes," Mia replies.

"What's amazing is how I've never seen it this way before. I mean, I used to think Sara was just a cold person," I say, nodding toward the girl behind the counter, "and now I see she doesn't even see me; she's not even present."

"Yes." Mia smiles warmly. "This is what it feels like to wake up to yourself. *The Truth is this newfound clarity you're experiencing is your natural state.* What you are noticing is how much people are actually living inside their own programming. Programming that's filled with worries and concerns about them not feeling good enough. They are not even present and they are not even aware they are doing it because they've been trying to survive ever since their original ego inception as a child. When our thoughts and feelings are no longer filled with misunderstandings or misconceptions, then we are no longer operating from inside our perception of reality, from our ego, we see the Truth, or Reality as it really is... meaning, we wake up to who we really are."

"Wow, I am amazed at how much I didn't see this before," I say, still in awe of this whole experience.

"Why would you?" Mia winks at me. "Fish don't see their own water."

Her words land with clarity.

"Are you ready Sue, to see *more* of who you really are?" Mia asks.

"Yes!" I say.

"Great! Yesterday, you got to see for the first time your ego — the false identity you created to survive your life when you thought you weren't capable of being with an experience that you'd never had happen before— the day of your ego inception. The great news is the more clearly you know who you are not, the more clearly you can now see who you are. *The first key to being unapologetically you is to become aware of who you really are.*"

Mia pulls out a diagram called "Who I am Thriving."

My New Empowering Decisions are:

Who I Am Thriving:
(The Authentic Aligned Self)

Potential

My New Empowering Attitude:

My New Role:

My New Behaviors/ Feelings:

My New Daily Actions/Habits:

What Will Be My Results, Now, From This Way Of Being?

© Mia Hewett Performance Catalyst, Inc. All Rights Reserved.

"*The second key to you being unapologetically you is to decide you are capable of being with any situation, even if you don't know how. The key is understanding that it's your decision, that you are capable, that has you trust your ability to be competent.* In a moment, I am going to have you take me back to that exact experience on the farm, but this time you are going to decide you are capable. Then I want you to feel for how you would be capable so that you get to experience the success of this same experience that was always available on the other side.

"How you know you've been successful is when this experience no longer has any feelings of resistance, judgments, or attachments, meaning you no longer think it should've been different or shouldn't have happened, but instead you find the gift this experience actually gave you. Then, and only then, will you have freed yourself from this self-imposed trap by evolving your consciousness to a higher state of newfound clarity.

"To support you in your success, I want to remind you of the wonderful Law of Polarity that says for a failure of an experience to exist, the equal and opposite success of that exact same experience must also exist in the same moment and time. Is this all making sense, Sue?" Mia asks.

"Yes, it does," I say.

"Ok, good. Now take me back through this experience, staying in the first person, but becoming an observer anytime you feel you need to pull back to gain a clearer perspective. Stay separate from your ego, and feel for how you would be capable – knowing that your ego will never feel capable, YOU are capable, as your real power always comes from inside of you – not in the situation or by trying to control another person.

"Now, hear what you heard, your father calling your name, and then hear what your father says, see what your father does, exactly what he did before, yet from a place of deciding that you are capable, what do you make this experience mean now? What's the gift you got from this experience?" Mia asks.

"Hmm, great question," I say. "Well, the first thing I can see is when I remove the emotional meaning I was giving it, I can see that I had been afraid of a lot of things before that day happened, and in my father's own crazy way, based on the way he was raised, I can see that he was probably thinking he was helping me because he wanted to toughen me up in order to make me stronger. You see, he was born and raised in Venezuela where he was raised to believe that the way you teach children how to swim is by throwing them in the water and letting them figuring it out. That was the way he was taught."

In saying that, I can see how I've made this whole experience all about me, when in truth, in his mind he was probably just doing the best he knew how. I just never saw it that way before.

"Yes," Mia says. "If you could truly put yourself in your father's shoes, where his past was your past, and his pain was your pain, and his level of consciousness, your level of consciousness, do you think that you might have acted like he did?"

The Truth in her words hit me like a ton of bricks. I had never thought about it that way before, and that Truth hurt a bit. In realizing this, I start to feel compassion and forgiveness for my father.

"Yes, I can see that now," I say.

"Is your father still alive, Sue?" Mia asks.

"No, my father died of cancer several years ago, and while I am sure his cigarette smoking was the cause of his death, I also believe he died due to his pain of regret. What I can see now is just how much I resisted my father my whole life, and so my whole childhood has been filled with these kinds of experiences. The irony is that even though I never became tough on the outside, like the way he had wanted me too, I did become resiliently tough on the inside." I smile, recognizing the True gift in this experience.

"Beautiful! That's an amazing gift," Mia says, "as real power is always invisible before it becomes visible."

"I can see that," I say.

"Now, knowing what you now know, being present to the gift in this experience what are the three new empowering decisions you make this experience mean? What do you make this mean about yourself, others, and the world, Sue?" Mia asks.

"I would decide to trust myself, because I do remember intuitively feeling that my father was up to something that he wasn't saying. Also, I would decide that I am smart and not confused. And that I can trust others, knowing that it's their actions that I have to pay attention to, not the words they say. I also, can see now that the world *is* safe because I can understand how it works, and that it's actually for me.

"Awesome, Sue! And what would be your decision now about being vulnerable and expressing how you really feel?" Mia asks.

"I am definitely deciding to take back my power by using my voice." I say, smiling feeling a deep sense of satisfaction in my gut.

"Great! Because what's the Truth about being vulnerable?" Mia asks.

"The Truth is that being vulnerable is what allows me to feel free," I say, realizing this for the first time.

"Yes! Because when you are vulnerable you are no longer keeping any part of yourself a secret for your ego to protect," Mia says.

I sit with what she is saying for a few moments and then nod my head.

"And as a result of making these new empowering core decisions, Sue – that you can trust yourself, that you are smart, that you can trust others knowing that it is in their actions, not their words, and the world is safe, and that to be vulnerable *is* freedom – what then becomes your attitude now about life?" Mia asks.

"My attitude is that of self-trust and resiliency," I say, feeling powerful.

"Awesome, and now from a place of making these core decisions – that you can trust yourself, that you are smart, that you can trust others knowing that it is in their actions that you have to pay attention too, and that the world is safe, and to be vulnerable is freeing, and your attitude is that of self-trust and resiliency – what now becomes the role you decide your going to take on in life?"

"The role of being a confident, bold, thought leader," I say.

"Great! And so as a result of your new empowering decisions – that you can trust yourself, that you are smart, that you can trust others knowing that it is in their actions that you are going to pay attention too, and the world *is* safe, and to be vulnerable *is* freedom, and your attitude is being one of self-trust and resiliency and the role you've decided is to be a confident, bold, thought leader – what would then become your new behaviors and feelings from this way of being?"

"My behaviors are that of being bold, taking calculated risks, seeing things in reality so I can make accurate decisions, feeling confident, happy and fulfilled," I say, smiling.

"Yes," Mia says and then asks, "From this new empowering way of being, realizing how capable you really are, knowing what you know now, how would this experience then be different that day, letting go of any resistance or judgment or attachment?" Mia asks.

"Well, I can see that I wouldn't have been so terrified of him. I might have even consoled him." I laugh now at the irony I am seeing. "As I can see he was just as terrified. I mean he didn't really know what to do. I just never noticed that before."

"Brilliant! You are seeing him as he really is, in reality, not in your perception of who you thought he was or wasn't."

"Wow, yes, I can see that. I would probably have said something like, 'Dad, I got this. I am capable of being really strong. What can I do to show you that I am? What if I was to earn money and pay for Henny Penny myself? " I say my eyes become wet with tears.

"Yes, and by responding and behaving that way notice how that would affect the outcome with your father that day? How might that situation have ended differently? Coming from that way of being."

"I think he would've listened to me," I say.

"Great. Because when you decide you are fully capable, and are not resisting or pushing against him, but you are acknowledging and becoming genuinely curious about how this could work, the outcome must shift." Mia smiles. "This is Law. It is the Law of Cause and Effect. Does this make sense?" Mia asks

"Yes, but why?" I ask.

"Because True power comes from inside of you; in you deciding you are capable, your response changes, which then affects your outcome because then there is nothing for your father to fight or push against, so he is then able to see himself fighting with himself," Mia explains. "As you own your power, coming from these new decisions that you can trust yourself, that you are smart, that you can trust others knowing that it is in their actions that you are going to pay attention too, and that you decide that the world *is* safe, and being vulnerable *is* freedom, and your attitude becomes one of self-trust and resiliency, and the role you decide to be is a confident, bold, thought leader and the behaviors and feelings you take on are in being bold, taking calculated risks so that you can see reality, making accurate decisions, and feeling confident, happy, and fulfilled- what would then be your actions and your daily habits coming from this way of being?"

I think for a moment and then answer, "I would take more action to be seen. Meaning, I would show up, speak at more conferences, stand out more, I would speak up more, and be on more podcasts and television shows."

"Yes! Yes, you would! So, can you see that it is in you deciding that you are capable that will then lead to your new decisions, your new attitude, which then will lead to your new role, which will in turn lead you to do these new behaviors and experiencing new feelings, which will then have you take these new kind of actions that will then give you what new results?" Mia asks happily.

"Ha! All the results I want!" I say, feeling enthusiastic and then adding "Me being my power, being a confident leader, making a difference in the world while making more money in less time." I laugh at how simple this really is.

"And so, can you see that it doesn't really matter whether what you're thinking is true or false? That in an all-inclusive universe whatever decision you make, whether wanted or unwanted, that you hold as your focus long enough and internalize it emotionally, will create your beliefs, and your beliefs will determine your attitude, which will determine your behaviors, which will then determine your results, which ultimately will become your life?" Mia asks.[15]

"Wow. I can see that," I say.

"Nice job. Your work now is to make this way of being so familiar that it becomes your belief. *The third key to you being unapologetically you is knowing how to have an unshakeable self-esteem.* Meaning, that you no longer feel not good enough, because anytime you think you are not enough, it is because you are looking outside of yourself for validation from others."

"Yes! How do I get rid of doing that?" I say.

Mia smiles. "It is actually less about trying to get rid of it and more about awakening to the Truth of the "enoughness" that is already inside of you. Anytime, you hear yourself saying things like I am not smart enough, I am not perfect enough, I don't have enough self-discipline, I am not making enough, I am not lovable enough, I am not likable enough, or any other version of not-enoughness, what you are really saying is *at some level you don't feel you are capable of being enough to achieve what you want.*"

"Yes," I say. "That's exactly how I've felt my whole life."

"So, when you're running that pattern of 'I am not enough' how will you ever know when you are good enough?" Mia asks.

"Hmm..." I think about that for a moment. "I don't think that I can until I decide, right?" I say.

"That's right, because that pattern in itself is a vicious trap!" Mia says, smiling. "And when you find yourself in a trap, Sue, what is the first thing you must realize?"

"That I am in it?" I say smiling.

"Yes! The way out of a trap is to first become aware that you are in it, so then you can pull back and go up and out and look down on it, which will give you the clarity to transcend it," Mia explains. "Once you're aware of it, you then must decide you're totally capable of resolving it.

As one of biggest mistaken beliefs people have is that they think *they will feel good enough when* they make more money, *when* they accomplish the next goal or milestone, *when* enough people like them or love them, *when* they find Mr. Right etcetera, as if the solution to being good enough is somewhere outside of them that they have to go get, find or figure out, versus that it is inside of them and is *a place from which to operate.*

"*The Truth is that* the feeling of not being enough has nothing to do with how successful you are, or how likeable you are, or how loveable you are as how many famous successful people have you heard of, that despite all their money and fame, *they've never felt good enough* from their unresolved emotional traumas, like Michael Jackson, Kate Spade, Anthony Bourdain, and Whitney Houston, just to name a few.

"*The Truth is all unresolved emotional traumas are healable.*" Mia says.

"Why did they not think it was healable?" I ask.

"Because once our mind has made the decision that "there must be something wrong with us" which comes from our original Ego Inception, no amount of outside recognition, money, or love will make this better because we are caught in a self-fulfilling trap, our own Chinese Handcuff, a misunderstanding or misconception that we've created and we forgot we created it.

"Our ego is running the show. But when we understand how to truly heal our emotional traumas, and then clear up our misunderstandings or misconceptions, that are in our way, we can then be free of them. Otherwise, we just end up repelling all others who try to tell us that we are good enough, worthy enough, or loveable by not accepting that we are.

"Because the internal decision has to come from us. *We cannot transform an inside problem with an outside solution.* And since we don't trust ourselves, others, or the world, we end up only questioning others motives, right? We think thoughts like, "Clearly there must be something wrong with you, if you can't see that there is clearly something wrong with me.'" Mia smiles.

"Ha! Yes, that's so True!" I say, smiling at just how many times I've actually done that.

"So, *have you* decided *to resolve your feelings of not being good enough, even if you don't know how?*"

"Yes!" I say.

"Great! Now, let's look at what is in the way of you being unapologetically you.

What's at the source of your insecurities, that is keeping you from feeling secure, confident, and more than enough?

"I had a client; we will call her Jan. And when Jan came to me, she was what society would call successful. She was super determined and driven, along with a fantastic work ethic, which is how she landed her current position. Having bigger goals is what kept Jan on track.

"However, she was exhausted and burnt out because everything was a fight. This constant battle was making her physically sick. She lacked energy and always felt like she was fighting against a current. She was the breadwinner in her family and had felt over time, that she had just become a machine of doing.

"Jan valued family more than anything yet she felt guilty that while she was physically there, she was rarely ever present. She was always worried about how she was going to hit her next goal. On top of all that she felt paranoid that no one liked her, because she felt like she didn't ever fit in. Jan never felt good enough or worthy enough and never really had any true friends. Jan knew she was limiting her potential, as she was doing so much, yet not making the progress she knew she was really capable of.

"The problem was that as a young girl Jan survived her life with her mother by walking around on eggshells every day. Even though Jan was now a grown woman, she was still emotionally six. She was trapped in the day she experienced an emotional trauma and created her Ego Inception. This emotional trauma was limiting her intellect and her true potential.

"After I supported her in seeing her Ego Inception, she could then see more clearly who she really was. When she no longer saw herself as her Ego, but as her true self, her self-image changed. She no longer ran the pattern of overthinking, or being anxious, she awakened and became present to reality and was able to now apply tactical strategies to her business. She was no longer being nervous around a certain kinds of people. She was now able to spend quality time with her family and developed an unshakeable self-esteem and self-image.

"Jan now actually owns her own business, she became unapologetically herself, and has gone on to make more money in less time, traveling and putting both her kids through college.

"So how did Jan get there?

"She first had to become aware and clear up the misconceptions or misunderstandings that were in her programming. Those she thought were True that simply weren't. As babies, we feel love and security when we are being held or hugged and if we are not held or hugged enough, we will literally stop growing and if this lasts long enough, even if we are fed all the right nutrition, we will die."

"Wow, that's amazing! I never realized how traumatic this could be for a baby," I say.

"Yes, as a child, we feel that we need the love and connection from outside of us and if we don't experience this from a parent, it can often feel like we don't exist or like we are going to die. And while it may be True as a child that your emotional wound is not your fault, as you didn't know you had the ability to be capable, your healing is hundred percent your responsibility as an adult. So, let's clear up the misunderstandings or misconceptions that are having you feel insecure so you can truly thrive, live your full potential, and develop an unshakable self-esteem. So you can be unapologetically you," Mia proclaimed.

"Yes, how do I do that?" I ask, excited to learn this.

"THERE ARE 3 HUMAN THRIVERS:"

Our self-esteem, which is how we see ourselves, and how much we appreciate our worth comes from how much love we allow ourselves to feel and how capable we decide to Be.
© Mia Hewett Performance Catalyst, Inc. All Rights Reserved

"The Truth is there are three Human Thrivers that create you having an unshakable self-esteem. The first Human Thriver is Love: When it comes to love, Sue, what have you been taught or come to believe love is?

"I used to believe that love was finding the right soul mate, finding the right person who would take care of me." I say reflecting.

"Yes, most people have been taught that love comes from the outside. The best examples of this were the Disney movies of our childhood. For example, Cinderella, Snow White, and Sleeping Beauty who all needed to be saved by someone else.

"The key in this misunderstanding is that this kind of love is coming from a need, something outside of one's self which can then feel like a burden, or a kind of tit for tat, or some form of manipulation which is our way of trying to compensate for a deeper underlying problem of not feeling good enough. So nothing ever feels enough as it can feel insatiable. Is this making sense?"

"Yes, it really does, as I can see that anytime I felt like I didn't matter or if I didn't feel like I was not the most important thing, then I didn't feel loved which would make me angry and then I would withdraw. I hated feeling dependent on my significant other for attention," I say.

"Exactly, and how this can show up in business is when we don't feel we are enough, we will feel undeserving of asking for money, because we won't adequately charge for our services, or we won't raise our prices to be more in line with the amount of value our services are actually providing. For some people this will show up in that they are only able to sell for other people, but not able to sell for themselves," Mia explains.

"Wow, I think you just described me to a T," I say.

Mia smiles. "What stops most people is their fear of being rejected because of their desperate need for people's approval. *When the Truth is that Love is an ever-present phenomenon as it is always available in any moment, at any time, just like the air we breathe.* We just have to make ourselves present to it. For when we are loving and appreciating ourselves it is easy to freely give and freely receive love, without conditions. To be clear, I am not at all saying you can't ask for what you would prefer because when we are operating from our alignment, asking for what we want *is* natural. It just won't feel like it is coming out of desperation. The last thing that's important for you to know about love is that *another person can only love you to the degree that they love themselves and you can only feel love to the degree that you love yourself. As love can only come from the inside."*

"That's so true," I say, seeing how mistaken I have been.

"Yes, we are either allowing love by being present to it or not. Check in for yourself... how many times in your past have you been angry, or upset, and someone was trying to love you, and you didn't feel any love?" Mia gives me a quizzical look.

I laugh. "Plenty," I say, amazed.

"Exactly. *The second Human Thriver is Security.* Most people see security as something they need, that's outside of them. What have you been taught or come to believe where your security comes from? How to feel safe in the world?"

"I was taught, mostly by society that there is a right way to live and a wrong way to live.

So to be safe and secure I had to go to school, get a good job that pays a lot of benefits so I can retire with a pension. And I knew that would take forever, as I wanted to be a fertility doctor. And for someone as poor as I was, that seemed like a pipe dream, as it would've taken me twice as long because I would've had to work, and go to school part-time. I then met, my now ex-husband and he had just started an insurance company and we had a lot in common, as we both came from poor backgrounds, and we both wanted to be successful," I say.

"So, in running your own company, how did you try and be safe?" Mia asks.

"I can see now, in hindsight, that our business wouldn't do well anytime we started operating from a place of survival. Like when we were constantly thinking, how can we cut back versus when we started to really gain momentum by asking ourselves how we could create more? That meant hiring more people before we actually knew how we were going to pay for them."

"Exactly! Operating from safety is one of the biggest psychological killers of any business because it has us making decisions from survival," Mia says.

"Yes, I totally agree. Because in hindsight it wasn't the one error we made, but it was the consistent errors we made whenever we focused on how wrong something was going instead of what was going right," I say.

"Yes, the biggest misconception or misunderstanding is that our security is coming from outside of us. When *The Truth is our Security comes from us deciding that we are fully capable, even if we don't know how* and then it's in us mastering this ability to make our decisions and then make our decisions right. That's what creates our life living intentionally by following all the way through to achieve our results.

"The Truth is you will only ever feel as safe and as confident to the degree that you believe that you are capable. Because when you believe you are capable, you shift how you see yourself, and how you see yourself *is* what's determining your results. *The key is in understanding that our results will not rise above how we see ourselves. To be unapologetically you, you must shift how you see yourself and then your results rise*," Mia says.

"So how do I do that?" I ask.

"By making the decision, deciding you are capable, and then turning your decision into a belief. How would you feel knowing you are fully capable of being with any situation, any person, and in any circumstance without ever losing your power?" Mia asks.

"Oh, my gosh, Mia, that would be amazing!" And then it hit me: "Wait, this is what I've always been looking for, and I didn't even know that I was looking for it until this very moment!"

"Yes, and let me guess; it's because you had the wrong problem?" Mia grins

I sigh. "Oh, my gosh, Mia. Yes! I thought it was outside of me. I thought I just needed to be with the right person, that somehow if I could just be with the right person or the right partner then I would feel safe, then I would feel powerful. Or that I just needed to figure it out like there is a right way to do something, and if I could just figure it out in the right way, then I would feel safe, then I would feel powerful. And now, I realize the reason I've never felt safe or powerful is because I haven't ever really believed I was capable."

"Yes, because you didn't *see yourself* as capable and powerful," Mia adds.

"Yes, that's right, I kept thinking that it must be something outside of me because deep down, wow, I can't believe I never saw this, because deep down, I thought I needed someone to save me," I say, amazed by this realization.

"Exactly, because in Truth the real problem was you didn't trust yourself, so you thought you needed someone else to save you, from you," Mia says.

"Ouch! I never saw how deeply I mistrusted myself," I say, now seeing it everywhere. I could see now how I didn't trust myself to make decisions, so I would avoid them by obsessively overthinking, I could also see how I didn't trust myself to achieve what I really wanted, so I would constantly look for more information or seek outside advice. I didn't trust that people really like me, so I never really got too close to anyone. I never really had any True friends and I didn't trust that Mr. Right wouldn't leave me, so I always had to leave first. I didn't trust that I was ever good enough so I didn't trust life," I say, astounded by the enormity of it.

Mia smiles at me.

"Just when I think I've cleared the biggest misunderstandings or misconceptions of my life, you help me clear even more! Ha! This is amazing." I laugh.

Mia smiles at me with warmth and compassion.

I am amazed at how this woman knows exactly what to say and when to say it, and when she knows not to say anything at all. I wonder if I will ever instinctively have those skills.

"*The third Human Thriver is Self-Esteem*: Where do you believe your self-esteem comes from?" Mia asks.

"Well, prior to meeting you, I used to think everything was coming from outside of me and now I know that's simply not true. But my first thought was that when others would approve of me or when they believed in me, or when they admired what I'd accomplished," I say, not enjoying hearing myself admit this out loud.

"Yes, most people have it that their self-esteem is based on what other people think of them, whether people approve of them or not, which only reinforces their feelings of not feeling good enough. This is all coming from their first emotional trauma-their Ego Inception. This leaves you trapped, caught in a Chinese handcuff, feeling like you need recognition to survive. Feeling trapped inside of a pattern of 'damned if you do and damned if you don't', which always has you end up feeling powerless. And there are people who will create drama in their experiences just to gain attention, because inside that trap some attention feels better than no attention at all.

"When in Truth, the word esteem literally means to appreciate the worth of. *True self-esteem, which is the secret to you feeling confident, comes from you deciding to appreciate your self-worth. To do so, you have to raise your self-image by raising your standards for yourself and deciding you are capable while being present to your infinite potential that is all around you.*

The question is, Sue, are you allowing yourself to feel worthy and deserving of everything and anything? Are you awakening to the Truth of your enoughness?

"Because deciding to live from your full potential is about having an attitude of self-ownership, not arrogance. *The key to Real Power and knowing your enoughness is Claiming It.* You just have to decide, for if not you, Sue, who could ever decide for you?" Mia asks.

"No one," I say, "I have to decide."

"Yes, the entire world is at your disposal and the surety is in you trusting yourself and claiming it! Fantastic work! I acknowledge your willingness and your courage to discover the Truth within you. You did an amazing job today! Now, your work is to live this every day. Meaning, become present to the Truth about Love, Security, and Self-Esteem until these are so familiar to you, that thriving returns to your natural state! Will you take that on?" Mia asks.

"Yes, Mia. I feel it, and I always want to feel this way," I say.

"Great, We will talk again!" Mia says.

With that, we set up our next meeting and she is out the door, leaving me to reflect on how much this one woman has changed my life in such a short period of time. I can't help but wonder how the world doesn't know about her yet? And with that, I grab my belongings and head out the door.

CHAPTER 8

HOW TO STOP USING FORCE AND START USING REAL POWER

"Mastering others is strength.
Mastering yourself is True Power."
– LAO TZU

"Yes, Mia, but how do I stop feeling like people don't really like me?"

We are back at our favorite hideaway: Café Susu.

"I mean, I have always felt different, like I don't fit in." I feel relief just expressing this out loud.

"I think it might surprise you that every single person I've worked with actually feels this exact same way," Mia says.

"Really? How's that possible?" I ask.

"There are three big obstacles that get in the way of most people being their power, trusting themselves, and being the force they were born to be.[16]

"The first big obstacle that gets in your way is your belief that you are separate from others. When your perception of reality has you believing you're all alone, your different, or that you don't fit in, you pinch yourself off from the flow of life that would have you feel connected, happy, and thriving.

"The reason you do this is because when you are raised in an environment where you don't feel safe, where you feel like you have to walk on eggshells because someone is either abusive or just plain moody, where you feel like they are constantly focusing on what you are doing wrong instead of what you are doing right, and your safety is dependent on them, their erratic behavior is what has you feel insecure because you never learn how to feel certain, secure, and capable. In your environment, with whom did you not feel safe?" Mia asks.

"My father," I say.

"And so how would you compensate for not feeling safe with him?" Mia asks.

"I would make every attempt to avoid him, or just try to please him in some way," I say.

"Yes, and do you remember doing certain behaviors that would give you some sense of control? Something you could be really good at? For a lot of my clients, it was that they could be really good in school. They felt they could control their grades."

I think about it for a minute. "Ha! I forgot about this, but I actually used to copy the encyclopedia. I can see why now because there was a sense of control in it as I felt like I couldn't get it wrong. I mean, it was the encyclopedia after all! That's the equivalent to Google; has anyone ever questioned whether Google's information is wrong?" I say, half-jokingly. "I just never knew why I did that, until right now."

"And so, can you see how this pattern of behavior would still play out in the todays of your life anytime you feel uncertain, like when you don't know the exact way to do something or don't have something to copy?" Mia asks.

"Wow, that's exactly it! I then feel completely lost," I say, shocked at how this was all connected.

"Yes, because your worst fear is that you'd be doing it wrong, because doing it wrong in your family would mean what?" Mia asks.

"Death," I say. "It would feel like I was going to die."

"Yes, because when you did something wrong as a child, what would happen?" Mia asks.

"I'd get the belt or something just as bad if not worse." I think back to how many times I'd survived life.

"Yes, so can you see how your brain linked pain and the fear of dying to anything that you might do wrong?" Mia asks.

"Yes," I say.

"That's because it is programmed to be on high alert, to protect you, and keep you safe," Mia explains. "The problem is, in reality, your father is no longer hitting you with his belt. Yet, your brain has it that he is and has you reacting to anyone who appears to be a threat like your father until you awaken to the Truth and shift this, emotionally, and then evolve your consciousness.

"This is because, as children when we don't feel safe, we learn to latch on to any little thing that we can do right as a way to have some sense of security, even when it's a false feeling of security. For some people, this false sense of power or control will show up in them as someone who is always getting angry. Or for some, it shows up in them becoming an abuser themselves, or they will become violent with themselves. For others it can show up in that they are always sad or always crying, or for some this false sense of power or control will show up in them using drugs or alcohol, or by always overeating.

"The key is in understanding that any self-deprecating behavior, meaning anytime you are disapproving of yourself by judging or criticizing yourself, you are attempting to regain a false sense of control by compensating for your feelings of being powerless. Consider, this is you trying to control life by surviving it.

"When you are feeling alone, or different, can you see that this is an attempt to control your situation, circumstance, or even other people?" Mia asks.

"Ouch! I never saw it this way before," I say, a little embarrassed.

"No judgment as this is a pattern we all run when we are trying to survive our lives, yet it is also the same pattern that will never allow us to thrive in our lives. What benefit can you see that you get from running this pattern? Because we only keep a pattern in place from which we're getting some form of benefit. So what benefit do you see that you are getting?" Mia asks.

"I think it's because I get to feel, in some sort of weird way, that I am also special in that I am misunderstood," I say.

"Yes, and if you are misunderstood, and therefore special, Sue, why is that a benefit?" Mia asks.

"I get to be alone and tell myself that no one gets me," I say, feeling a kind of satisfaction.

"Yes. And if you get to be alone and acknowledge yourself, that no one gets you, why is that a benefit to you?" Mia asks.

"Hmm." I repeat her question again in my head: Why is getting to be alone a benefit? "I think it's because I get to feel right about it."

"Yes! That is the real benefit of why you do this. *The second biggest obstacle that gets in the way of you believing in yourself and being your power is your need to be right.*"

As soon as she says it, I can feel the Truth in her words.

"The power you feel by wanting to be right is but an illusion of control, and your real power comes from the freedom you will feel in letting go," Mia says. "The misunderstandings or misconceptions you have are in not understanding that this false sense of power is coming from your ego, which is why it's limited. Ego is always coming from self-preservation, which means it will never have you thriving or ever leave you feeling fulfilled and satisfied, but will only have you feeling more alone, more isolated, and more like you are right.

"The Truth is you are so connected to life that you would be dead without this ever-present connection. It's just that when you are in your perception of reality, and not reality, you can't see it as one can't see the forest for the trees. Just like a fish to water.[17]

"The way out of feeling alone, different, and like no one really likes you is to locate the source of what's triggering you and causing you to withdraw from reality. Meaning what has you feel separate and alone?" Mia asks.

"I feel that way anytime I feel someone's judging me," I say.

"Great, what do you think their judgment means?" Mia asks

"It means that in some way they don't approve of me. Like I am not doing something right," I say.

"Yes, and what do you see is the misunderstanding or the misconception in thinking that they need to approve of you for you to do it right?" Mia asks.

I think deeply about this. "That I could ever know exactly how to do it right for every single person, as everyone is different?" I say, "That's a big misunderstanding!"

"Exactly, why is that a big misunderstanding? How does life really work? From the outside-in or inside-out?" Mia asks.

"The inside-out!" I smile, seeing my misunderstanding.

"Then what's the Truth about whether someone likes the way you are doing it or not?" Mia asks.

"Ha! The Truth is I just have to like it myself." I laugh at how funny it seems in hindsight.

"One hundred percent!" Mia smiles. "Your work is to turn your liking yourself into a belief. Which would be your new emotional set point. Because it is in you liking yourself first that allows you to stay present and connected to reality and not to lose your power. Only then can you influence all others to their power."

"But how do I not react to their judgments? How do I not feel crushed?" I ask.

"*By realizing that people's judgments are based in their own limitations and their own perceptions of reality.* Then you can understand that the real reason you are reacting is that their judgment causes you to question and judge yourself because you are not sure about you. Your negative feelings are always your indication that the thoughts you are thinking are out of alignment from that which you desire. Meaning that the thoughts you are feeling are hitting up against your own limitations, your own limiting beliefs, misunderstandings or misconceptions. They're hitting your own rules or past traumas that you have not yet resolved.[18]

"So in Truth, the negative feelings you are feeling, in reality, are just a gift that your emotional guidance system is actually working, as it is letting you know that the thoughts you are thinking have an origin that is ready to be healed.

Which is *exactly* what's happening inside of people, and why they are being triggered, and are in their own judgment," Mia says.

"But Mia, I have done years of therapy," I say. "I thought I've healed all of this."

"Most people think that if they've talked about it and are aware of it, that it should be enough to heal it, but in Truth, Sue, if you are still being triggered, emotionally, then nothing has really shifted in reality. So therefore you have not healed it," Mia explains. "The way you know if you have truly healed it is when you no longer have any feelings of attachment, resistance, or judgment with this type of experience. Then and only then, you have truly set yourself free! This is why, in Truth, there is no such thing as cutting people out of your life, because when you are still thinking about them, and therefore emotionally still being triggered by them, in reality you are just reliving it over, and over, again. So, in Truth you have to love them to release them. This can only be done once you have cleared away the misconceptions or misunderstandings that's separating you from this Truth."

"So, Mia, are you basically saying that their judgments are based on their own limitations, and my reactions are based on my judgments of my own limitations? I'm feeling a bit confused."

"Yes, each doesn't know what they don't know, and each can't see what they can't see, so it appears like the disagreement is with the other person, when in fact it's within ourselves. As there are, in reality, no others." Mia winks at me. "As we are all just living inside of our own programming. *The Truth is we are each getting exactly what we believe, not what we say we want because our beliefs are equal to our vibrational emotional set point.* And in an all-inclusive universe, where everything is energy, there is no such thing as 'no' as we are either emotionally resisting or reacting, so consequently, we are creating more of what we do not want. Or we are emotionally aligning and agreeing, so therefore we are creating more of what we do want. Either way, in an equal opportunity universe, we get more of what we focus on as it is Law."

Mia takes a photo out of her gold folder called "When We Hit An Internal Block" and lays it on our table.

"What's actually happening is you're getting stopped by their judgment because there is something in you of which you don't believe you are capable. And anytime you do not think you are capable of being with a person, or situation, or a circumstance you will either want to fight—by attacking and defending, by trying to become more than human, which is superiority ego – or you will want to flee – by freezing, being confused, or trying to please, by trying to be less than human, which is inferiority ego. Either way, it's still your ego, which means you are limited and have no real power.

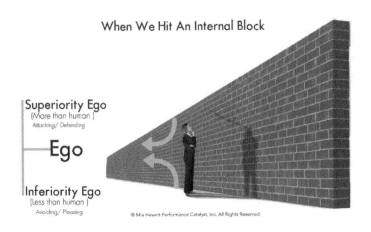

When We Hit An Internal Block

Superiority Ego
(More than human)
Attacking/ Defending

Ego

Inferiority Ego
(Less than human)
Avoiding/ Pleasing

© Mia Hewett Performance Catalyst, Inc. All Rights Reserved

"And there is another way, but you will have to give something up, first."

"What?" I say, curious at what it could be.[19] [20]

"Control," Mia says, smiling. "Because it will take the opposite of control, which is for you to let go and become genuinely curious. Anytime you feel triggered, I want you to stop, pause, pull back, and go up and out by becoming like a fly on the wall looking down on the situation becoming genuinely curious. This allows you to access your potential and power by gaining greater clarity on the situation and then being able to respond once you've found your alignment. *This is what you must do to shift and operate from a higher consciousness.* The way out of your ego is for you to decide to no longer blame others for your own feelings, but to look deeper at the gifts your feelings are pointing at, knowing that anytime you feel negative emotion, it always means that there is something of which you don't think you are capable.

The Truth always sets us free, because the only thing any of us ever need to be set free of is our own ignorance."

Right then, a young girl who works there walks over and proceeds to fill my water glass. I am grateful for her timing. While there are many things I value, being ignorant is not one of them. I take a drink of water, digesting Mia's words realizing how much I thought was True that wasn't. It's humbling.

I am not sure how long I sat there drinking, but when I finally become present I say, "Wow."

"Amazing, right?" Mia says.

"The third biggest obstacle that gets in your way of you being your power, and being the force you were born to be is that you have never been taught where your feelings are actually coming from. Meaning, you are not aware of how you operate. Have you ever thought about where your feelings are actually coming from, Sue? Mia asks.

"Hmm, I want to say from other people, but I now know that's not True. Then I want to say from the situation that's happening, yet after today that doesn't sound right either. So I feel like it could only be from inside. Right?" I ask.

"Yes. And after today can you see what's been dictating your feelings?" Mia asks.

"My thoughts?" I say.

"Yes," Mia says, "Because your thoughts are coming from what's in your subconscious programming. This is because as children our conscious minds haven't fully developed before the age of seven we only have a subconscious mind. With just a subconscious mind our brains were very much like sponges absorbing and downloading everything that was going on around us in our environment as if everything were True, even when it was not. This is where you got your worldview from, your fixed ideas, your evaluations, all which have made up your opinions about life, which you then internalized in your emotions, becoming your beliefs- Your perception of reality.

"We all went on to download behavioral programs by observing our parents, our siblings, our peers, and other people around us. These experiences then became fixed, and hardwired, like on a video recording program, in our mind. This video recorder, which we weren't even aware existed, has been going around automatically downloading programming. This programming is who we think we are — our ego identity, and we will then run this programming for the rest of our lives, until the day we awaken and decide to take ownership of it.[21] [22]

"Does that make sense?" Mia asks.

"Yes. I had never thought about our minds being like a video recorder before," I smile.

"Yes, on average ninety-five percent of the time, your thoughts are just coming from your subconscious programming, which are then dictating your feelings. Your feelings are then dictating your experiences. Your experiences are then dictating your programmed behaviors, which then dictate your actions, which are then creating your results," Mia explains.

"So in Truth, can you see who you are really fighting against when you are feeling bad?" Mia asks.

"My own programming!" I say, a bit shocked.

"Yes!" Mia says excitedly.

"Wait a minute, Mia. Are you saying that every time I have felt bad, that at that moment, it was because I was fighting against my own programming?"

"Yes. For instance, when you have a desire to be liked, which is coming from your conscious mind, and then you have an experience where you feel judged, you react because your subconscious programming only has a program from a past experience where you decided you were unlikable. So you suffer because you become out of sorts within yourself as your desire to be liked is hitting up against the contradiction in your own programming. This is the way our human mechanisms work."

"So how do I make all my minds work together?" I laugh, feeling like a person with two heads.

Mia laughs. "By aligning your emotions with your thoughts by first feeling for how you would like to feel. For example, the feeling of being likable, feel what it would feel like to be likeable and feel likable. Now, reach for thoughts that align with that feeling," Mia instructs.

"Yes, that feels good," I say, "I could think thoughts like, it feels good to be me. I like being me, I like that I grew up in Venezuela and I see beyond people's skin colors, I like allowing people their own opinions as I have my own opinions. I really like that about myself."

"Excellent! That's alignment. Alignment is when what you think, what you say, how you feel, and what you do are all in alignment. Now your work is to turn this process of alignment into a habit. A subconscious program that will run automatically without any effort, like brushing your teeth."

"So how do I do that?" I ask.

"The best way for you to do this is to develop this as a small habit by setting three daily alarms — for example, one in the morning, one in the afternoon, and one at night. The alarm is for you to check-in with yourself, stopping whatever you are doing in the moment, becoming aware of where you are operating from... Are you in your ego? Or are you in your aligned self? And if you find yourself in your ego, let go by being forgiving of yourself. Then without any judgment, choose the feelings you'd like to feel by reaching for thoughts that feel good to when you think them. This will have you instantly find your alignment causing you to shift your emotional set point. Does that make sense, Sue?" Mia asks.

"Yes, I say.

"By consciously paying attention to your feelings, and by shifting your thoughts, you'll develop the habit of moving yourself vibrationally, emotionally, and instantly. This allows you to no longer feel like a victim to your feelings because you'll be operating from a higher state of consciousness. This is real power. Because the fastest way for you to decide your future is to build the habit of that future, right now. It's when we don't understand where our feelings are coming from that we limit our successes, our potential, and our overall happiness, because we are not aware of the power we have, in every moment, by intentionally aligning ourselves.

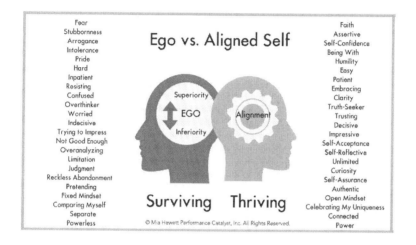

"The key in this understanding, Sue, is for you to become aware of where you are operating from, without judgment. When you are in your ego, you are in a destructive consciousness. When you are in your potential, you are in a constructive consciousness.

"Looking at these two different operating states, what percentage of your day do you think you are operating from your ego?" Mia asks.

"More than I want to admit," I say, trying to not self-judge, but judging myself anyway.

"Yes." Mia smiles. "When we cut off all our escape routes, and we put ourselves in a position where we have to face ourselves, we grow, and that's when we rise. The bridge for you to go from a destructive consciousness to a constructive consciousness is by letting go of your judgment and being forgiving of yourself. Because when you are forgiving of yourself, you become present with reality. And when you are present with reality, you can then choose the operating state in which you want to be in.

"What would be the value of you letting go and being forgiving of yourself for judging yourself for having operated more of your days from your ego, Sue?" Mia asks.

"I would move myself to feeling better right away," I say.

"Yes, and can you feel how that would instantly give you power?"

"I can," I say.

"It's when you begin to affirm you can do this that you've got this. By being able to consciously and emotionally move yourself to a constructive consciousness, you build back your self-trust, your trust in others, then your trust in life, and you become the force you were born to be."

"Yes," I say, feeling it.

"And notice when you stay in the emotion of self-trust. How does this shift the way you see life?"

"Well, I am no longer looking for what is wrong. I am more accepting... it feels rather peaceful," I say, observing my feelings.

"And when your self-trust becomes your new emotional set point, your natural programming," Mia adds, "then how easy would life be?"

"I imagine pretty easy!" I say.

"Yes, because when you operate in alignment, with who you really are, and you are in flow with life, rather than resisting or pushing against life, you produce what others would call miraculous results, but what you have come to understand and know as your natural birthright," Mia smiles.[23] This is because when we trust ourselves, Sue, we feel fully capable, we feel non-judgment, non-resistance, and non-attachment to people, situations, or circumstances-we are *Truly Free*. This is the freedom everyone's really looking for. Freedom from their own ego, their own limitations, their own myths, their own subconscious beliefs and the magic all starts with letting go!"

And just like that, she gets up, gives me a big hug, and is once again out the door, leaving me to simmer over all that had just transpired.

CHAPTER 9

HOW TO USE YOUR POWER TO CREATE YOUR REALITY INTENTIONALLY

"By banishing doubt and trusting your intuitive feelings, you clear a space for the power of intention to flow through."
— WAYNE DYER

As I sit in silence in the café, hushed by the big snow that is quietly falling outside, I am reminded that in the bigger scheme of life for everything there is a season, that these seasons represent parts of our lives, and when we can pull back far enough, we see the beauty that was always there laying in the silence.

"Hi, Sue! How are you?" Mia asks, startling me out of my deep reflection.

"I'm good!" I say, "I was just reflecting on how much you've taught me over these past few weeks and how much I am now able to see the beauty in all things."

"Great. Tell me more?" Mia asks.

"Well, like how I can see more of what's behind what someone is saying, so I am not taking things personally. I am not reacting, you know, or trying to please everyone," I say, seeing the difference in myself.

"I love this!" Mia says, clapping her hands in a celebratory manner.

"And it's also bittersweet, as I know today is our last session and I am really going to miss this!" I say, wondering how I am ever going to live without her.

"But, I do have a question for you, Mia. You said last time that the magic is in letting go, and I can see now where I've been addicted to controlling things." I laugh at myself and then add, "I can see now that I do this as my way of trying to feel safe, but Mia, if I just let go, wouldn't I be giving up?"

"Great question, Sue!" Mia says, smiling at me. "*One of the biggest obstacles that stands in the way of most people creating their reality is allowing exceptions*, which means, allowing yourself to come up with reasons rather than being fully committed to your outcome. This is a result of not valuing yourself and therefore not valuing your word. *The key is in you being fully committed to having what you want, yet not being attached to how or with whom you will achieve it.* This isn't about you working harder or trying to control your outcomes, as it is *more* about how to work smarter by intuitively trusting your feelings to get exactly what you want-intentionally.[24] *The Truth is you will have to give up relying on your intellect and be open to trusting your intuition.* For example, Julie had the same question you did when she wanted to create $30,000. And in the past, this would've taken her working about six months to get those kinds of results. She asked me, based on what you're teaching me, how can I create $30,000 in less time, if time is an illusion? So the first thing I did was help her come up with a plan on exactly what problem she would solve to create this income, I then supported her in finding the feeling place of already having $30,000. Her work then was to hold this result adding a sense of urgency.

"Not an urgency out of desperation, or neediness, but an urgency for a bigger cause, her being her full potential... Julie decided she wanted to create this money so she could be able to move into a new place. Now her work was to get into alignment everyday feeling like she already had this result and then for her to take inspired actions by trusting her intuition. She decided she would create this in ten days or less, letting go of how or with whom this would happen. Julie ended up creating this in seven days," Mia says.

"How did she do it?" I ask, eagerly anticipating the answer.

"Every day for twelve minutes, three times a day Julie would get into alignment with her vision of already having this result, seeing herself living in her new place, using all of her senses feeling what it would feel like to experience this just for the joy the experience gave her. Then she would let go of any thoughts on how or with whom it would happen, and from her alignment, she would ask herself 'who should I call? Who is the best fit for what I solve?'

"And one day her intuition told her to reach out to a particular woman and her intellect told her, 'No, that woman doesn't have the money to work with you,' yet she followed my teachings and trusted her intuition, being fully committed to her results, without being attached to how or with whom. But when she spoke to this particular woman, she didn't feel that the woman had a big enough dream that she could help her fulfill. Then all of a sudden, she felt the woman's energy change, and then the woman said, 'Oh! I am sorry, my boyfriend just got in the car with me.'

"Feeling like that was her cue, that she needed to go, Julie said, 'Ok, awesome. Well, I want to leave you with one last thought before you go, and that is for you to consider that your familiar routines, and approaches, are all traps! Meaning, to live your potential you must be willing to give up your 'faith in the familiar' to develop your ability to have the unfamiliar result.' And with that, she heard a man laugh, and the woman said, 'Oh, I am sorry, that's my boyfriend, and he's a bit of a skeptic.' To which Julie replied, 'Great! I used to be a skeptic too! Hey, from one skeptic to another, may I offer you something?' The man replied, 'yeah.' Julie says, 'You really want to begin to question and become really skeptical about all the things you keep doing that are only giving you *more* of the same results. You want to become really skeptical about those things!' To which her boyfriend laughed, and then responded, 'I like you, I want to talk to you,' so they set a time to talk the next day and he was the one who hired her. That is how Julie created $30,000 in seven days.

"So, Sue, the answer to your question, is never giving up your result, but having to let go of how you think your result should actually happen. This takes you trusting that you have all the power but none of the control because your potential will never be found in your intellect.[25] Does that make sense Sue?" Mia asks.

"Wow! It does, I really see how her intellect was saying no, not to call the woman, but her intuition said yes. I love that story," I say.

"Exactly, *in life the very thing that got you to where you are will not get you to where you want to go*. Letting go of your intellect will allow you to see opportunities you wouldn't otherwise seen. Have you noticed that anytime you've gotten the results you've wanted, or something even better than expected, that it came from you not resisting, or pushing against, what you didn't want?" Mia asks.

"I have!" I say, smiling at the Truth, "But I thought in those times it had only happened because of luck. I mean luck favors the prepared, right?"

"It isn't luck that has you achieve what you want, Sue, as everything in the universe is operating in an orderly uniform way. The sun comes up every day, and it's not on your to-do lists. Gravity *is* gravity without any of your own doing. Our hearts beat, even while we are asleep, and we don't have to take turns waking up to pump each other's hearts. And like these unseen forces that are governing our lives, call them God, call them forces, your decisions cause your thoughts, and emotions, which create your behaviors and actions, which in turn create the effects that results in you having the life you have. *The key is understanding that this is all happening naturally and orderly, not randomly.* In order to maximize your potential, you must be willing to let go of trying to use raw effort or sheer willpower to achieve your dreams and instead learn to think in an orderly way, going with the flow, trusting in these unseen forces and invisible resources as they are the easiest and most powerful resources available to you. *This is the power of aligned intelligence."*

"Ok, on that note I have another question for you, Mia, when it comes to making money," I say.

"Sure! Shoot!" Mia smiles.

"As a child, my mom always told me that I could do anything I put my mind to and I believed her, yet I can't understand then why was I so poor," I say, curious to how she sees this.[26]

"*The prerequisite to having what you want is always a decision.* So, consider, that what you thought was a belief, that you could do anything you put your mind to, was really a mere wish or hope, as most people have never been taught how to create a belief on purpose but are creating unconsciously by default. Because the Truth is you cannot help but create. In fact, everything that you have that you don't want is of your creation; it's just that you didn't know that you were creating it.[27]

"In order for you to create a belief on purpose you have to hold your focus and thoughts on an idea, imagining all the delightful details as though you've already achieved it, internalizing it as an emotional set point, by finding the feeling place of it and giving it a meaning, and then acting in alignment with your desire. Meaning that you then act in complete faith as if you knew your success was guaranteed by behaving with total conviction that what you think, what you say, how you feel, and the actions you take are all in alignment, such that you see yourself this way, until your dreams becomes realized in reality," Mia explains.[28]

"What's interesting to me, Mia, is as I hear what you are saying I can now see that what I was actually doing was thinking a few happy thoughts, but then I was really feeling poor," I say, realizing the difference.

"Exactly, your feelings of being poor are what were actually showing you what you really believed, what your emotional set point really was, as everything is energy, and we always get what we believe," Mia says.

"I can also see now that somewhere along the line I believed I either had to be a dreamer – like my mother – or I had to be realistic – like my father – but somehow I didn't think I could be both. Somehow I felt that I had to choose one or the other. I can also see where I believed that I could either be a really nice person, helping people, or I had to be realistic and do what needed to be done by forcing people to do things that I wanted them to do in order for me to make money. And because I never wanted to be *that* person who forces, like my father, I never had any money. Then at twenty-one I met a man, who had just started an insurance company, and he was definitely the more practical, realistic kind, and I was still very much the dreamer, so together we created an amazing team. In hindsight, I believe it's because we balanced each other out." And then it hits me! My mind is blown. "Wow, I just got why I've felt so lost! It's because I never realized, until this very moment, that I didn't believe that I could actually win without him, because I had never truly decided to own my success!"

"Amazing awareness! So what's the Truth you see now?" Mia asks.

"Somehow I still had it in my mind that practical business people were takers, and I didn't want to be known as a taker because all I've ever wanted was to be a giver," I say, my eyes welling up with tears.

"Yes, any time we run a pattern where we have a desire for something but have a belief that contradicts it, we suffer until we awaken to the Truth," Mia says.[29]

"Yes," I say.

"So, what's the lie you see now?" Mia asks.

"I can see that the lie is that I thought that *all* business owners were takers, or were people who use force to get what they want, much like my father," I say.

"Yes, and what's the Truth you see now?" Mia asks.

"The Truth is that's not the only way to do business," I say, smiling, proud to make money and be a giver.

"Great. So what would you need to do, Sue, to align both those worlds within you?" Mia asks.

"Hmm... that's a great question. I would have to see myself having exactly what I want, truly serving people, meaning really being straight with people, allowing their shit to come up, and not really make it mean anything about me, to help them achieve what they want, which in turn allows me to achieve what I want. So, basically, I would be being a dreamer who delivers win-wins, in reality," I say, laughing at myself for making this so difficult.

"Bing! Bing! Bing!" Mia acts as if I have just won a huge prize! "That's the Truth. Sue! That's you – operating in your full potential, being in alignment with you.

"Yes!" I say, smiling at how far I've come in our time together.

"In Truth, our decisions about ourselves are what define us, and then we act according to those decisions whether we are aware of them or not.

"Many years ago, Sue, I was having a conversation with billionaire Martin Franklin. At that time he owned the Jarden Corporation, which he ended up selling a few years later to Rubbermaid for about $14.3 billion dollars. And I was asking him, as a billionaire, how does he overcome fear?

"And he said, 'I don't have fear, Mia, I do my work thoroughly, and then I make a decision. I try to address the downside, but I never second-guess my instincts, while I remain open to the critique. The most frustrating thing is people who can't make a decision, and leadership is all about making decisions. It is really easy not to be effective if you are not making decisions. I am just so driven to make sure it works that once I've made the decision, I don't think about how much money I am going to lose if I make the decision wrong, I think about how much money I am going to make when I make the decision right,' Mia shares, smiling.

"Wow, I never realized just how important our decisions really are," I say, hearing this story.

"The problem is most people have never been taught how to make a True decision. So often when you don't get the results you want in life it's because you think you made a decision, when in fact what you have only really done is just said you'll try.

"Notice where this has shown up in your life; think back to an experience where you see that you missed an opportunity or didn't get the result you wanted, and consider that it's because you really hadn't gone *all in.*"

"Meaning that some part of you, in either what you were thinking, or what you were saying, how you were feeling, or the actions you were taking or not taking, was out of alignment with your desire. There was some part of yourself holding back, or you had one foot in and one foot out the backdoor, not really playing full out," Mia explains.

"Yes, I can see exactly when I would do that when I would start to feel uncomfortable. I would get distracted, or let someone talk me out of my idea," I say, noticing the pattern.

"Great awareness," Mia says. *"Your work is to make a decision and then make your decision right by altering your beliefs to come up to the level of your desires. In other words, you must go all in.* Look for yourself, how would you know if you've made a True decision? What would be different in your reality?" Mia asks.

"I am not sure but I know something would have to be different," I say.

"Yes!" Mia says, smiling. "A True decision will shift reality. Meaning, your mindset will shift, your priorities shift, your calendar shifts, your behaviors shift, your checkbook shifts, and your activities shift as you have shifted by going all in. This is the difference between living life, intentionally, versus aimlessly. *To live intentionally-is to shift reality.*

"So, what do you see has been keeping you from operating intentionally?" Mia asks.

I laugh. "Definitely think it's from being stressed and overwhelmed."

"So, I have to ask you, Sue, what is stress?" Mia asks.

"I've never really slowed down to think about that," I say, reflecting.

"Since all feelings come from our own thinking, what are the thoughts you are thinking that then show up as stress?" Mia asks.

"I guess thinking... I don't know how I am going to do it all so I get confused about where to even begin," I explain.

"Great, I want you to consider that confusion is not natural. Meaning, you were not born confused. As a baby, you may have cried when you wanted something, but confusion is a social conditioning brought on by trauma. Looking back in your life, when did you decide to start running the pattern of confusion? Or is it a pattern you are modeling from your childhood? Is this your Father's or your Mother's pattern, or maybe both?" Mia asks.

"It feels like they both ran this at times, but I can clearly see now that I started running it the day my chicken died," I say, never realizing this before.

Mia pulls out a piece of paper called "Traumatic Experience."

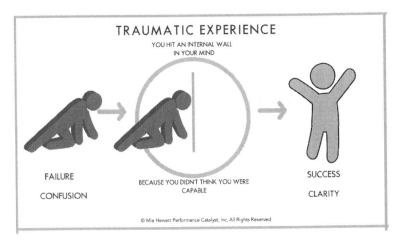

TRAUMATIC EXPERIENCE

YOU HIT AN INTERNAL WALL
IN YOUR MIND

FAILURE

CONFUSION

BECAUSE YOU DIDN'T THINK YOU WERE
CAPABLE

SUCCESS

CLARITY

© Mia Hewett Performance Catalyst, Inc. All Rights Reserved.

"Consider that day, you went into an experience that you never knew could happen before. You hit an internal wall in your mind because *you didn't know how* to be with that experience, so you retreated in your mind. Your way of coping with this trauma has been to control it by becoming really stressed out, confused or overwhelmed. Can you see how you do this as a way of protecting yourself from anything you don't think you are capable of being with?" Mia asks.

"Wow! I never saw I was doing that," I say, feeling both amazed and confused.

"The reason you have not been able to solve this problem is that all along you have had the wrong problem. *You thought the problem is you don't know how,* right?"

"Yes," I say, more confused.

"I know you are confused; this is a good thing as I am scrambling and rewiring your brain right now. Stay with me. You are doing great!" Mia says smiling at my confused state. "You see the real problem, Sue, is *you have never decided to be capable.* You have to decide you are capable, first, before the how will show itself. Meaning, the way will come after your decision.

"So, can you see the reason you keep getting stopped, stuck, and struggling is you've been trying to solve the wrong problem? You've been looking for *how to do something before you've actually decided to do it.* Which is not the way life works."

"So, I am not really a confused person?" I ask, my brain still feeling a bit mushy.

"No. You are a normal person who has been trying to cope because you have the wrong problem. Can you see that anytime you feel stressed, overwhelmed, and confused it only means one thing?"

"That I don't think I am capable," I say.

"Yes. So the first thing you must do to heal this trauma is decide you are capable, even if you don't know how. Are you ready to decide you are capable to heal this pattern?" Mia asks.

"Yes," I say, not fully aware how, and trusting the process anyway.

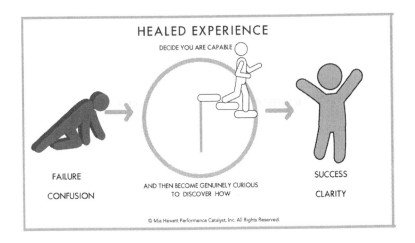

"Great. Now, I want you to feel and internalize what feeling capable would feel like. For example, the day you decided you were going to ride a bike, even though you didn't know how, or the day you decided you were going to tie your shoes, even though you didn't know how. Feel for what it would feel like to decide and feel capable, even though you don't know how."

"It feels amazing," I say.

"Exactly! Where do you feel it?" Mia asks.

"In my gut and then all over," I say.

"Perfect! Now, become genuinely curious, and ask yourself if you could be capable, how would you be capable? And what does your intuition tell you?" Mia asks.

"I would tell myself I got this. It's all working out for me, even if I don't know how. I don't need to know how. I got this," I say, feeling a sense of peace in my body.

"Good. So if you are not a confused person, who are you?" Mia asks.

"A very clear person," I say.

"Yes, yes, you are, as clarity *is* natural," Mia says, smiling. "And as a clear person, who's totally capable, who would you be being letting go of this trauma, while keeping all the gifts you've learned from it?"

"I would be a force!" I say, grinning. "I would be unstoppable."

"Yes! That's who you really are! One last thing about feeling overwhelmed. Overwhelm happens as a result of us trying to think about too many things at one time or beating ourselves up for thinking we could actually get everything we think about done in a day. The Truth is billionaire Martin Franklin has the same twenty-four hours in a day that we do. The most important thing for you to become aware of is where are you operating from -Your ego or your aligned self?" Mia asks.

"My ego," I say with certainty.

"Exactly. And anytime you are in your ego it only means what?" Mia asks.

"That I don't think I am capable," I say.

"That's right. *Your ego will never feel capable,* as it is coming from your false self.

"The Truth is you can never get everything done, and you don't need to in order to be successful *as success is not a game won by those who do the most, but by those who focus on the least*. Meaning by narrowing your focus and pigeonholing exactly what you want to be an expert in and then focusing on the least, by simplifying and prioritizing your day, keeping the end in mind, how different would your life look, Sue, if you were operating intentionally, every day, versus operating by default, or in overwhelm?" Mia asks.

"Oh, my gosh! It would be totally different!" I say, laughing out loud seeing how different I would look.

"*Yes, as you can never hit a target your not aiming at.*"

"So, how do I live this way?" I ask.

"*By living intentionally each segment of your day.* The best way to do this to develop the habit of using your brain as a tool that it was designed for rather than letting it be the master of you.[30] To do this, what you want to do is get into alignment at the beginning of each and every day by getting really clear on what your intended outcome is for each time segment of your day.[31] For example, before getting on a sales call, come from the end in mind by asking yourself what's my highest and best intention for this call? Connect to your certainty as the expert and hold the intention to only work with clients you can genuinely support in achieving the result you know how to achieve, letting go of all other attachments. This will allow you to stay connected to your power having the clarity and presence to see exactly where they are, and where they want to be, while letting you recognize the potential of something when it is not quite right, ensuring every opportunity for it to go the best way. This is you being in alignment with you making the most out of your time and money by knowing what's most important, having it go in the direction that is in the best interest of everyone involved.

"This is a powerful process of defining the end in mind as a way of pre-paving and cleaning up anything that could get in your way that you may not be consciously aware of so that you slow down, to reflect, and then be able to speed up. This is you operating more deliberately from your potential, as you will then have the opportunity to choose, on purpose, the thoughts and the feelings that you do want. In time, this practice becomes so natural; it will become a natural state, a place of rhythm and flow, from which you operate.

"This allows you to create consciously your future experiences, which gives you real power over your future segments as you are projecting your expectations into your future, understanding that *what you expect is always realized*. This is you using your power to create reality, intentionally, trusting yourself, others, and the world.

"*Now that we have debunked your myths, uncovered your blind spots and supported you in understanding how the Universal Laws work and how you can work more effectively and efficiently being in alignment with these laws, you are now able to become MORE of who you really are. For you have forever shifted your relationship with yourself, others, the world, your potential, and therefore your success. How are you feeling now?*" Mia asks

"I want to stay in this newfound experience forever. I want to milk the newness of this for all I can experience," I say, smiling and feeling a tremendous love. "I also have a tremendous amount of compassion, not only for myself, but for people everywhere."

I look at Mia... her expression says it all. She has tears of joy in her eyes and she hugs me tightly. I feel so much gratitude for this woman I have only just met and who has forever changed the trajectory of my life.

"The universe is a living breathing presence, Sue, that is inherently always moving toward more life and a fuller existence. In this universe, everything is alive, aware, and responsive. *Life* is *meant for more. Your work is to keep up with your alignment and be the fullest expression of yourself just like an oak tree that grows inherently and consistently to its fullest extension of itself.*

There is a great story I read once about Jigoro Kano, the founder of Judo where according to the legend, as Jigoro Kano approached his death, he had asked his students to bury him in his white belt. The highest-ranking martial artist of his discipline took on being a beginner beyond his life, because to him the journey of mastery is never over.

"Enjoy the journey, Sue, for the pursuit of mastery is not in just doing your best but in the ever-evolving journey of self-discovery of what being *more* of your best would look like."

With that, we say our goodbyes, we hug, and she is out the door.

I stand there in a complete state of joy and gratitude wondering how did she learn to help so many people shed the weight of their lives in such a short period of time?

And then I laugh as I hear her voice in my head say, *Alignment*.

I am eternally grateful.

Thank You!

*"A spiritual awakening is when something emerges
from within you that is deeper than who you thought
you were. So, the person is still there, but one could
almost say that something more powerful shines
through the person."*
— ECKHART TOLLE

Thank you! I feel so much appreciation that you've read this book!

This is the beginning of a life-altering, joyful, fulfilling way to live from your Aligned Self.

The fact that you've gotten to this point in the book tells me something beautiful about you, that you are ready to become *more* of who you really are. You're ready to thrive spiritually, mentally, emotionally and physically to achieve the results you have always dreamed of more than at any other time before.

Although this journey took me over fifty-one years to unravel, I want you to have all the shortcuts that will debunk your myths and clear up the biggest misunderstandings or misconceptions that are keeping you stuck, stopped, and struggling, so that one day we can all look back and say, "What glass ceiling?"

To support you in awakening to your potential and feeling instantly better mentally, emotionally and physically, I created the *Meant for More* Assessment just for you.

It is a simple diagnostic assessment that will help you get crystal-clear on which areas you need to shift to come more into alignment, mentally, emotionally and physically to be your power. The bigness and boldness of who you really are, connecting you to your inner strength, your inner wisdom, your inner beauty, and your True power so you too can be *a force to be reckoned with.*

To thrive now, go to
www.MiaHewett.com
or for more information, email me at
mia@miahewett.com
as I answer each email personally.

Also, keep in touch and share your successes with me by joining me on Facebook or Instagram as I am passionate about your results because you living your full potential is what gives me one of my greatest joys.

Acknowledgments

To my mother and father who gave me a life full of contrast and adventure so that I could eventually come to know myself fully.

And especially to my mother, who has always told me I could do anything I put my mind to. I am forever grateful for your endless love and support- your editorial skills! LOL!

To my sisters, who've added so much color and joy to my life. You mean the world to me.

To my children by birth and by marriage, Sierra, Dale, and Ashley.

While "I am not perfect, I have always had perfect intentions." May this book support you along your journey in discovering me newly, discovering others newly, and seeing yourselves without your childhood conditioning of who you think you are.

Within these pages lie the keys to achieving everything you want in life and it all starts with the most important and longest relationship you will ever have – that with yourself.

To my ex-husband for teaching me the practicalities of business and for loving me even when I didn't know how to love myself.

To my amazing partner, Michael, for being on this journey with me and for consistently reminding me of the importance of play! Thank you for allowing me the space to fully discover who I am.

And finally, to all my clients, for trusting me with your deepest most personal secrets and for having the courage and the willingness to face yourselves to achieve your multitude of successes!

You inspire me!

Because of each one of you, I am *more*.

Thank you, from the bottom of my heart!

About the Author

Mia Hewett is a human potential expert. She has co-owned and operated a seven-figure business, is an international speaker, and a world-class business coach. Mia is the founder of Aligned Intelligence™ or A.I.M., a methodology that removes all blind spots, fear, anxiety, and self-doubt to have you feel empowered, make accurate decisions and work smarter, not harder to maximize your results and live your potential.

Mia's method is for those wanting to achieve self-mastery.

Like many of you, Mia's most significant source of pain was knowing she was meant for more, yet not understanding why she kept secretly struggling to achieve it.

Mia's excited to let you in on what successful people know that they often cannot explain by helping you bridge the spiritual or conceptual awareness to a practical understanding in a way that makes it easy for you to implement.

Now she lives an incredible life, living her life's purpose and doing what she's most passionate about, and you can too! Mia has run all five major world marathons and currently lives in Boston and Florida with her partner, Michael, and their French bulldog, Buddha.

About Difference Press

Difference Press is the exclusive publishing arm of The Author Incubator, an educational company for entrepreneurs – including life coaches, healers, consultants, and community leaders – looking for a comprehensive solution to get their books written, published, and promoted. Its founder, Dr. Angela Lauria, has been bringing to life the literary ventures of hundreds of authors-in-transformation since 1994.

A boutique-style self-publishing service for clients of The Author Incubator, Difference Press boasts a fair and easy-to-understand profit structure, low-priced author copies, and author-friendly contract terms. Most importantly, all of our #incubatedauthors maintain ownership of their copyright at all times.

Let's Start a Movement with Your Message

In a market where hundreds of thousands of books are published every year and are never heard from again, The Author Incubator is different. Not only do all Difference

Press books reach Amazon bestseller status, but all of our authors are actively changing lives and making a difference.

Since launching in 2013, we've served over 500 authors who came to us with an idea for a book and were able to write it and get it self-published in less than 6 months. In addition, more than 100 of those books were picked up by traditional publishers and are now available in bookstores. We do this by selecting the highest quality and highest potential applicants for our future programs.

Our program doesn't only teach you how to write a book — our team of coaches, developmental editors, copy editors, art directors, and marketing experts incubate you from having a book idea to being a published, bestselling author, ensuring that the book you create can actually make a difference in the world. Then we give you the training you need to use your book to make the difference in the world, or to create a business out of serving your readers.

Are You Ready to Make a Difference?

You've seen other people make a difference with a book. Now it's your turn. If you are ready to stop watching and start taking massive action, go to **http://theauthorincubator.com/apply/**.

"Yes, I'm ready!"

Endnotes

[1] "Coyotes are the ultimate American survivors. They have endured persecution all over the place. They are sneaky enough. They eat whatever they can find – insects, smaller mammals, garbage... [they are] extremely flexible and adaptable to different kinds of environments." – Darryl Fears quoting Stanley D. Gehrt, an Ohio State University professor and wildlife ecologist who runs the Urban Coyote Research Project, which studies coyotes in the Chicago area.

https://www.washingtonpost.com/.../heres-why-there-are-so-many-coyotes-and-why-the...

[2] **Even Billionaires Make Mistakes:** Like most successful people, billionaire Ray Dalio, who has an estimated net worth of more than $17 billion, has learned more from his mistakes than his successes. His most painful mistake occurred in 1982 when he correctly predicted the credit crisis, yet incorrectly bet that the markets would go down instead of up. Mexico then defaulted on his loans, and Ray Dalio had to lay everyone off except himself, almost bankrupting his company. Instead of quitting and going back to a comfortable Wall Street job, he chose to learn from his mistakes and ensure Bridgewater would succeed, which it has for the past thirty-plus years. He said, "Every time you confront something painful, you are at a potential important juncture in your life – you have the opportunity

to choose healthy and painful truth or unhealthy but comfortable delusion."

[3] **Case Study:** I once had a client who came to me, as she wanted support in living her full potential. She said, "I am struggling! My mother died six years ago, and ever since she died, I haven't been able to get it together." And I said, "That's not True." She said, "Mia, I don't think you understand. My mother was everything to me, she was my world, and because she died, I've always been struggling." I said compassionately, "This is not True." To which she replied. "Mia, my mother died and I am struggling. What cannot be true about that?" And I said, "The Truth is your mother died. She died *one time*, and in your mind, you've made her die every day for the last six years. The Truth is she died. The reason you struggle because you think she shouldn't have. And anytime we go against reality we will struggle."

[4] **"Time isn't precious at all, because it is an illusion.** What you perceive as precious is not time but the one point that is out of time: the Now. That is precious indeed. The more you are focused on time – past and future – the more you miss the Now, the most precious thing there is." – Eckhart Tolle

[5] **Distinction:** Learning to Memorize vs. Having A Conscious Level of Awareness & Understanding.

- *Learning to Memorize* comes from school, where we are taught that if we read something, remember it, and then are able to recite it back then that is enough to know it. When the truth is, we just have a conceptual understanding of it, yet knowing something, as a concept, is not enough to get a result.

- *Having a Conceptual Understanding of something is not the same as living it.*

- *Having a Conscious Level of Awareness & Understanding:* to live it, you would have to embody it by being consciously aware, understanding, and then having had experiences to be able to apply it with any person, situation, or circumstance to achieve your results.

[6] Distinction: Intellect vs. Intelligence

- *Intellect* is often considered to be related to "facts" or the cognition and rational mental processes gained through an external input. The knowledge we know is often based on misconceptions and misunderstandings.

- *Intelligence* is related to internally aligning by "feeling" for your alignment intuitively.

[7] **The Power of a Misconception/Misunderstanding:** WHile there are many misconceptions and misunderstandings that have been passed down from generation upon generation, here are just a few:

- *Epilepsy* was viewed for over 3,000 years as a result of a person perpetuating evil doings or as evidence of possession by demons.

- *Bloodletting.* For over 2,000 years the withdrawal of blood was believed to prevent or cure illness.

8 Distinction: Reality vs. Perception of Reality

- *Observing Reality*: When we take a big picture view of an experience by viewing it as if we were a fly high up on a wall, without giving a meaning or significance to what we are looking at, so we are separated from it, then we have access to looking at reality as *is*.

- *Perception of Reality:* When we are in the details of an experience and we are perceiving it, not as it is, but as we are, based on our past programming, our worldview, our preconceived ideas, our beliefs, our judgments, and our thoughts, attaching meaning and significance to those experiences. This is why two people can see the same thing, and yet perceive something very different about it.

9 **Reality Check:** Our results will never exceed our expectations.

Why?

Because of our reticular activating system (RAS).

Once our mind has accepted or rejected an idea, whether it is true or not, our RAS will immediately begin to filter out any irrelevant information based on the decision we made and will then only focus on relevant information that supports our decision.

Good or Bad. Wanted or Unwanted.

The problem is our RAS is a filter, yet it has no filter for the Truth.

In other words, you get to prove yourself right, even when you are wrong, because just because you believe it doesn't make it True. It just means you believe it.

[10] **Case Study:** Before Jack came to work with me, he had never made more than $1,000 a month consistently in his network marketing in over five years. He didn't believe he could really get people to follow him. Jack's attitude was that he didn't believe in people, that he felt people were a waste of his time. He didn't believe he was capable of acquiring what he wanted. He often felt alone, frustrated, anxious, and depressed. This was causing a huge strain on his relationship with his girlfriend. He wasn't prospecting, as other things would constantly distract him, and then he would call the same people over and over again, listening to motivation audios to just absorb more knowledge. When he decided to work with me, I took him through my Aligned Intelligence method, and within two months he was making $4,600 consistently. A 400 percent increase. But best of all, for the first time he believed in his worthiness and his capability. He became a confident leader of people, as he believed he now had what it took within him. His attitude became one of "working with a purpose." His feelings were that he was "the light" and being this light, he became a real contribution to others which had him feeling selfless versus selfish. Jack's behaviors were all about authentically prospecting to those who had a problem he knew he could help them solve. He put systems in place and leveraged his team and has now trained others to be confident leaders as well. His girlfriend was so impressed that she joined him in his business, he proposed, and they are now soon to be married.

[11] Distinction: Perfection vs. Self-Mastery

In interviewing and working with so many *uber*-successful people, there is one characteristic that stands out the most with all successful people and that is that they've all decided that discomfort is the key to their self-mastery. This is very different than pursuing perfection.

- *Perfection:* is a self-sabotaging loop because, at its core, it is an attempt to gain people's approvals, which is a self-limiting pattern.

- *Self-mastery:* at its core is a decision to be the best version of yourself, which is unlimited, as you continue to stretch what you think you are capable of.

When Tony Robbins was interviewing Michael Jordan, he asked, "Michael, you are known as the greatest basketball player that ever lived. How did you do it?"

Michael went on to explain that he always demanded more from himself than what he ever thought he was capable of. Michael said, "Tony, the reason I was able to beat them is they were competing with me, and I was only competing within myself."

[12] Epigenetics by Bruce Lipton, Ph.D., *Author of The Biology of Belief: Unleashing the Power of Consciousness, Matter, and Miracle*

Dr. Lipton discovered that things are not what they seem. Nor are they what he was teaching in medical school or what he was lead to believe.

"Our health is not controlled by genetics. Conventional medicine is operating from an archaic view that we are controlled by genes. This misunderstands the nature of how biology works...

"Medicine does miracles, but it is limited to trauma."

"The AMA protocol is to regard our physical body as a machine, in the same way, an auto mechanic regards a car. [...] The problem is that while they have an understanding that the mechanism isn't working, they're blaming the vehicle for what went wrong. [...] They don't take into consideration that there is a driver in that car. [...] In essence, if you do not know how to drive you are going to mess up the vehicle."

[13] The Counterintuitive Way of Getting out of a Tailspin.

Real power is not about force; in fact, it is the complete opposite and is why force will always eventually succumb to real power. In August of 1912, Lieutenant Wilfred Parke was flying his biplane during the British Military Aeroplane competition when due to his human error his plane went into a tailspin. To try and recover from this tailspin, Wilfred tried increasing the engine speed and pulling back on the stick to no avail. It was common knowledge back then if a pilot found themselves in a tailspin, death was certain. Wilfred's aircraft descended 450 feet as spectators braced themselves for the fatal crash when Wilfred did something completely counterintuitive. He applied the full right rudder, which leveled it out at fifty feet allowing him to land safely. The "Parke's Technique" was then created. Yet many more pilots would go on to die because their natural impulse was to pull back on the stick until 1914, at the beginning of World War I when pilots began to receive this counterintuitive training which would go on to save many lives.

¹⁴ Ego by Eckhart Tolle

"All the misery on the planet arises due to a personalized sense of 'me' or 'us.' That covers up the essence of who you are. When you are unaware of that inner essence, in the end, you always create misery. *It's as simple as that.* When you don't know who you are, you create a mind-made self (the ego) as a substitute for your beautiful divine being and cling to that fearful and needy self. Protecting and enhancing that false self (the ego) then becomes your primary motivating force."

¹⁵ How to Create a Belief on Purpose

The great news is your beliefs are not fixed! Because your beliefs are just habits of thoughts that you keep thinking. Have you ever noticed that some of the beliefs you used to have as a teenager are not the same beliefs you have today? The Truth is just because you believe it, doesn't make it True, it just means you believe it. Whether you want to create a belief on purpose or whether you've created a belief by default it takes the exact same process:

1. You first have to hold your focus on a thought or idea consistently enough that you internalize it emotionally and give it a meaning.

2. You then have to feel it emotionally, in your gut, so it becomes an internal emotional set point.

3. Then you have to make this feeling place so familiar that it becomes how you see yourself, so that every time you think that thought, you feel that feeling, and you see yourself that way!

That's how you'll believe it — as that is how any belief is formed.

[16] **Loneliness Epidemic:** In the last fifty years, **rates of loneliness** have doubled in the United States. In a **survey** of over 20,000 American adults, it was found that almost half of the respondents reported feeling alone, left out, and isolated. Further, one in four Americans shared that they rarely feel understood, and one in five people believe they rarely or never feel close to people.

Loneliness is the subjective experience in which a person feels solitary. When we become aware and then understand why we feel alone and how we have used this pattern in order to survive our life, we can then choose to run a different patter that will have us thriving in our life. The Truth is the illusion is we are separate when in reality we are so interconnected. What separates us from this Truth is the misunderstandings and misconceptions we have picked up along the way and how we have used our Ego to comforted ourselves anytime we didn't think we were understood never learning how to stay in our power, stay present, and be capable to get the success of our experience which is on the other side.

[17] **How Connected Are We Really?**

We are all interconnected. As people, we are dependent on our environment for food, clean air, water, fuel, clothing, and shelter to live. Plants are what give us the very oxygen we need to breathe. By using the energy of sunlight, plants can convert carbon dioxide and water into carbohydrates and oxygen in a process called photosynthesis. As photosynthesis requires sunlight, this process only happens during the day. We often like to think of this as plants `breathing in carbon dioxide and `breathing out oxygen. The Key is in understanding that we are all so interconnected that if we were to be without one of these things all life would end. The Truth is there is only connection; the illusion is there is separation.

[18] How the Fears we don't Face Become Our Limits

Consider in our society, we are not taught how to face something stressful or uncomfortable, and move through it. We are taught either directly, or indirectly, to avoid it, attack it, or become numb and paralyzed by it. We think being uncomfortable means "there is something wrong." But what if being uncomfortable actually means something is right and on the other side of your discomfort lies the freedom you are actually seeking? A lobster is a soft, mushy creature that lives inside a hard shell. The hard shell does not expand. So how does a lobster grow?

As the lobster grows, its shell becomes really uncomfortable. The lobster will then go under a rock formation to protect itself, cast off its shell, and develop a new one. It will then continue growing, and expanding, and eventually, become really uncomfortable and confined, only to then once again go under a rock formation and shed its shell and start this process all over again. The key point is the very catalyst that causes the lobster to grow is discomfort. Without the discomfort, the lobster would not shed its shell, and therefore never grow. The key in understanding that the discomfort you face becomes your limit until it is no longer what limits you. The truth is we are our own glass ceilings and the very feelings that we've been taught or have learned to suppress, withhold, avoid, or defend "are" what is our internal guidance system telling us it's time to shed our rigid shell.

[19] Case Study: A Million Dollar Skill Set

When Dave was referred to me, he was the CEO of a rapidly growing company. To have the capital they needed to further the expansion he needed to sell a location.

Before opening up this new company Dave was a well-known figure in the community, and it was vital for him to succeed.

With this new expansion and growth, he needed to pull it together to execute.

He wanted support in getting his mind right, learning how to work smarter and not harder and being more strategic.

The problem was he was only used to operating from crisis mode.

He always struggled between doing the polite thing, the nice thing, or losing it by going off which he knew was holding him back and limiting his potential as he would get stopped with internal and external walls, and missed opportunities.

After a few sessions, we cleared up the misconceptions and misunderstandings he had, and then he learned a new skill set for any time he felt himself go into trying to be nice or feeling like he was about to be controlled or was going to lose it.

He would stop, pause, pull back, and then become genuinely curious which allowed him to then access his potential and power by gaining greater clarity. Then, and only then he would respond once he found his Alignment.

The next day that skill set made him a million dollars.

He was in negotiations to sell one of his locations, and the attorney for the purchaser had sent him a scorching letter degrading him in the letter. Rather than reacting from anger which he would've done so many times in the past causing him to miss out on opportunities, this time he stopped, paused, pulled back, found his clarity. In clarity he decided not to respond to the letter but, instead, he got an instinct to pick up the phone and call the buyer.

On the phone, Dave came from a position of certainty and curiosity, which caught the buyer off guard, as Dave was not reacting but was being genuinely curious.

Dave expressed to the buyer that he had done everything they had asked him for and was even willing to support this buyer in understanding the documents he sent him on the profit and losses. Dave then basically said to the buyer, you know if this doesn't work for you, then no problem man, we can just go our separate ways, as there were other buyers interested in this location, the buyer then said, no, no, no and Dave then closed a Million Dollar Deal.

[20] **Case Study**

When Derrick first came to me, he was having some success, just not the success he wanted. He worried if he would ever reach his goals and wondered if he was even good enough.

He would see all these uber-successful people around him and he would be frustrated and even angry that he didn't know what he needed to do to achieve those kinds of results, or even where to begin.

During our time together he ended up creating over a 200 percent return and went on to become #2 in the State of Florida in his company.

How?

No Ego whatsoever. Meaning when he stopped operating from his Ego. He realized that he was judging his appointments based on their titles and money.

Meaning, if he felt *superior* to their titles and money, then he'd *talk down* to them.

If he felt *inferior* to their titles and money, then he'd feel the need to *prove himself* to them. His need to Be Right was blinding his effectiveness with people and costing him a fortune.

By breaking down his ego, he was able to recognize and own that he was *capable* which gave him the certainty and confidence to no longer feel the need to have to prove himself.

He became someone who operates from 100 percent transparency and authenticity, which is what has made him unstoppable.

[21] "The *subconscious mind* is a database of programs and the *conscious mind* is connected to The Collective Consciousness of the World. The Conscious Mind is running the body, essentially like sitting in front of the computer and pulling up programs to run your lives. The Conscious Mind can create but it creates through the filter of Subconscious Programming."

– Bruce H. Lipton PH.D. Author of The Biology of Belief: Unleashing the Power of Consciousness, Matter & Miracles.

[22] **We Master Success by Mastering Our Minds.**

How you understand and use your mind is what will predict how successful you will be.

- *The subconscious mind,* also known as our habit mind, is designed to download and maintain our programming, our learned behaviors and to resist change. I.e., Learning to walk. Which is a good thing, as every morning when we wake up we instantly remember how to get up out of bed and walk, without having to re-learn this every day.

- So, every habit we have is related to a subconscious program. This means that whenever you get triggered, our subconscious mind will automatically fire off your programmed behavior. *As we operate ninety-five percent of our time in our subconscious programs.*

- *Our conscious mind* is what gives us our ability to evolve from being just reactive to being reflective. It also gives us our ability to choose. This is where our "free will" comes from. This is different from our subconscious because it is creative in it can choose to accept or reject an idea where our subconscious mind just follows a program.

The key in this is understanding that whenever we feel triggered by a stimulus subconsciously, It is our conscious mind that gives us the ability to *change our response to it, at the moment.*

Yet, if we are not aware or understand we can do this we will only operate five percent of our time *consciously.*

Mastering your mental self-care is what will allow you to go beyond mindfulness to effectively change your circumstances, to increase your creativity, allow your emotions to work for you versus against you, having you experience overall intellectual and emotional experience.

23 Is The Secret To Ultimate Human Performance The F-Word? By Steven Kotler

Flow is a thoroughly transformational experience.

Research shows that on the other side of the state, we're more confident, capable and aware. Even better, as was learned from **one of the largest psychological studies ever conducted**, the people who have the most flow in their lives are the happiest people on Earth.

Flow's effects on performance are both very real and really astounding.

In a **10-year McKinsey study**, top executives reported being five times more productive in flow.

This is a 500% increase. This means, if you spend Monday in flow, you can actually take the rest of the week off and still get more done that your steady-state peers.

While most of us spend less than five percent of our work life in flow, if that number could be nudged up closer to 20 percent, according to that same McKinsey study, overall workplace productivity would almost double.

[24] Distinction: Working Harder vs. Working Smarter

Working harder is what happens when you are not aware of how and where you are operating from; your Ego vs. Aligned Self and you have a belief that nothing that is worth having is easy.

- *Working harder:* comes from the unconscious belief that I have to try harder to prove I am good enough. Not only is this limited as you will eventually hit a point of diminishing returns, but eventually you will burnout, which most often shows up in weight or health issues, as you are trying to mentally and physically do it all. It's the constant feeling of swimming against the current.

- *Working smarter:* comes from consciously knowing your worth and being present in your listening to harness the environment around you, leveraging the value you provide, while tapping into infinite resources. It's a feeling of following the flow vs. trying to create the flow. This is about following the path of least resistance, as it is more about trusting your intuitive feelings.

- The difference between these two comes from the difference between operating from Habitual Thinking vs. Accurate Thinking.

- Habitual thinking is what has us making decisions inside our own perception of reality which is based in our misconceptions and misunderstandings, and past traumas.

- Accurate thinking, on the other hand, can only be accessed when you are fully present with reality, which is real power.

[25] Distinction: Intellect vs. Intelligence

- *Intellect:* is often considered to be related to "facts" or the cognition and rational mental processes gained through an external input. The knowledge we know which is often based in our misconceptions and misunderstandings.

- *Intelligence:* is related to internally aligning by "feeling" for your alignment intuitively.

[26] How Unresolved Money Patterns Limit Our Life

Before Michelle came to work with me she had hit a plateau in her business and in life. No matter how hard she tried she always seemed to just make enough money to get by, never really thrive, and Michelle knew she was meant for so much more.

During our work together Michelle shared with me that as a little girl her family never had any money and she heard her parents talking about a prominent businessperson in their society who had a lot of money. Hearing this, Michelle made a decision that she was going to grow up and make a Million dollars!

She was so excited she couldn't wait to share it with her mother thinking how excited her mother would be to hear this too! Only to experience, the sheer look of disgust and horror on her mother's face when she shared her excitement.

Her mother told her, "Michelle we are not those kinds of people."

She was raised to believe that people who have money were "ungodly." Not spiritual. As a result of this experience, Michelle only always had just enough money to get by and always felt guilty any time she wanted to spend money on anything that was just something she wanted until we healed this emotional experience and cleared her misconceptions or misunderstandings about money.

Michelle discovered the Truth about money is that it is an exchange of value for solving a problem. The bigger the problems the more money people are willing to exchange for its value to solve it.

Michelle learned that it is actually ungodly not to receive and allow God's blessings. She stopped being a blessing blocker and has gone on to make more money than ever before.

27 The Little Girl Who Decided To Create A Pony

When my daughter was young, I told her that she could achieve anything she put her mind to. When she was about five years old, she read the book Black Beauty and decided immediately she was going to have a pony

Not just any pony, but a black pony with a white diamond on her forehead. *Now, I have to tell you I thought this was really sweet and wonderful at the time, but I also knew I had no intention of buying a pony as we had two horses and one that she could ride, hence no need to have a pony.

I told her that if she wanted a pony, she would need to create the pony herself, as I had no intention of buying her a pony.

So, she asked me to remind her exactly how she can create what she wants. I then appeased her and explained you have to decide you already have her, imagine the feeling place of her, and then expect her, as what we expect is always realized.

And to my amazement... she did just that within less than ten days, she created that pony!

How did she do that?

As the Law would have it... I always got our horses hay and horse supplies delivered to our house, but this one time in all the years of ordering, they had forgotten the fly spray I ordered and the flies were really bad as it was summertime in Colorado.

We had to go into town to the feed store to get the fly spray.

While I was grabbing the fly spray my daughter sees a black and white photo next to the register of a pony and yells, "Mommy, mommy, that's my pony I've been talking about." I look and see this picture of a dark pony with a long mane and tail, and the phone number to call. My daughter sees the number and says call them mommy, as this is the pony. I reluctantly am thinking 'there is no way this is that pony because it doesn't have a white star, and since it's a black and white photo, for all we know it could be brown, but I call to show good faith. A woman answers and I ask about the pony and she says she is only five minutes down the road from the feed store so would we like to come to look at her? I said well I don't really have any intention of buying a pony but my daughter is insisting that this is the pony she has been thinking about. We go to the woman's property and the pony, who is all black, is in a round corral and my daughter goes right up to the corral and the pony comes over to her. The woman, shocked, says, "That's really interesting. She never usually comes over to people." Then the woman asked my daughter would you like to go in the pen and see her? Of course, my daughter said yes, and then while my daughter is petting this pony, she rubs her forehead, which moved the black main from the pony's head, and there on her forehead was a white mark shaped in the form of a diamond! In my shock I said, I really have no intention of buying a pony and the woman said well it seems like this pony likes your daughter so much that I am willing to sell her to you for only $500.00.

I couldn't believe it, but my daughter could.

We bought that pony that day and to date, we still have that pony as she is now twenty-four years old enjoying out her days grazing with a pack of other horses in a 160-acre hay field.

[28] How to Create a Belief on Purpose

The great news is your Beliefs are not fixed! Because Beliefs are just habits of thoughts that you keep thinking.

Have you ever noticed that some of the beliefs you used to have as a teenager are not the same beliefs you have today?

The Truth is just because you believe it, doesn't make it True, it just means you believe it.

Whether you want to create a belief on purpose or whether you've created a belief by default it takes the exact same process:

1. You first have to hold your focus on a thought or idea consistently enough that you internalize it emotionally and give it a meaning.

2. You then have to feel it emotionally, in your gut, so it becomes an internal emotional set point.

3. Then you have to make this feeling place so familiar that it becomes how you see yourself so that every time you think that thought, you feel that feeling, and you see yourself that way!

That's how you'll believe it – as that is how any belief is formed.

[29] I am not a sinner. I am a saint.

When Maria came to me, she was filled with self-judgment. She always felt like she was not as good as others, and consistently feared what others thought of her, she was afraid of doing it wrong, and never felt good enough or not worthy enough. She was also afraid of standing out, of being *really* good, or being seen, so she always stayed just under the radar, playing it safe, as she "didn't want to rock the boat."

She would always "just make enough money" so "I don't feel that I am asking for too much."

Maria had grown up in the church.

She struggled inside watching with envy other leaders living the life she desired.

Maria secretly wanted to claim her power and believe she could achieve anything her heart desired. Yet, she also believed that if she claimed her power that would mean she was saying, "I know better than God."

Key Understanding: Anytime we have a desire for something yet hold conflicting beliefs we struggle and don't achieve our results, since in a battle between our emotions and our logic our emotions will always win.

Through our work together she freed herself from believing she was a sinner, she stopped feeling guilty about all the things she thought she should be doing, like always reading her bible, and became present with God as a living, breathing experience.

This released the burden she had been carrying, that she had to be perfect (to try and prove she was good enough, since she was a sinner). She realized, inside, she had already accepted Jesus as her savior so she was now free to be a saint, completely and exactly how she was and is *as a perfect imperfection.*

Her *alignment with this is what caused her to fully step into her power,* to be an authentic leader serving others, she went from trying to make connections to finding it easy to connect with other leaders feeling like she was one of them, she became clear on who she was, she started traveling the world, leading others, and is on her way to building a legacy fund that will help others, who don't have the resources, know they are loved, and they can live the life they desire!

[30] **Distinction**: Multitasking vs. Focused Closure

- *Multitasking is a myth!* The truth is that multitasking is actually *impossible* – we don't do multiple things at once; we actually shift between different tasks quickly. This is what I call milkshake multitasking, which causes literal neurochemical chaos in our brains, which, in turn, causes literal brain damage. Milkshake multitasking switches confusion on in our mind and brain!

- *Focused Closure:* Starting from the end in mind, developing the disciplined habit of being intentionally and purposefully by directing your attention in a deeply intellectual way on each task to focused closure per task. This will have you operating effectively and efficiently, resulting in having peace of mind.

[31] **Parkinson's Law** is the adage that work expands so as to fill the time available for its completion.

In 1955, Cyril Northcote Parkinson, a British historian, wrote this in an essay in *The Economist* on his experience in the British civil service where he explained if something must be done next week, it would be done next week.

If something must be done tomorrow, it'll be done tomorrow.

Meaning we tend to plan based on how much time we have, and when the deadline approaches.

Serial billionaire Peter Thiel uses Parkinson's Law when building a company by asking, "How can we achieve our ten-year plan in the next six months?" Parkinson's Law is best used not as a way to have unreasonable deadlines but as a way to narrow your focus, get creative, approach things differently, and to get unconventional results.

NOTES

NOTES

NOTES

NOTES

NOTES

NOTES

Made in the USA
Columbia, SC
13 May 2020